BAZOOKA
VS
PANZER

Battle of the Bulge 1944

STEVEN J. ZALOGA

First published in Great Britain in 2016 by Osprey Publishing,
PO Box 883, Oxford, OX1 9PL, UK
1385 Broadway, 5th Floor, New York, NY 10018, USA
E-mail: info@ospreypublishing.com

Osprey Publishing, part of Bloomsbury Publishing Plc

A CIP catalog record for this book is available from the British Library

Print ISBN: 978 1 4728 1249 0
PDF ebook ISBN: 978 1 4728 1250 6
ePub ebook ISBN: 978 1 4728 1251 3

Index by Rob Munro
Typeset in ITC Conduit and Adobe Garamond
Map by bounford.com
Originated by PDQ Media, Bungay, UK
Printed in China through World Print Ltd.

16 17 18 19 20   10 9 8 7 6 5 4 3 2 1

Osprey Publishing supports the Woodland Trust, the UK's leading woodland
conservation charity. Between 2014 and 2018 our donations are being spent
on their Centenary Woods project in the UK.

www.ospreypublishing.com

Acknowledgments

The author would especially like to thank Kurt Laughlin, Timm Haasler,
Kevin Hymel, and Darren Neely for their help on this project. All photos are
from the author's collection unless otherwise noted.

Editor's note

For brevity, the traditional conventions have been used when referring to
units. In the case of US units, C/9th Infantry refers to Company C, 9th
Infantry Regiment; 2/9th Infantry refers to the 2nd Battalion, 9th Infantry
Regiment. The US Army traditionally uses Arabic numerals for divisions and
smaller independent formations (2nd Infantry Division, 741st Tank
Battalion), Roman numerals for corps (V Corps), spelled numbers for field
armies (First US Army), and Arabic numerals for army groups (12th Army
Group). In the case of German units, Arabic numerals are used for companies,
e.g. 3./SS-PzRgt 12 refers to 3. Kompanie/SS-Panzer-Regiment 12. Roman
numerals are used for battalion-level units, e.g. I./SS-PzRgt 12 refers to
I. Abteilung/SS-Panzer-Regiment 12.

Title-page photograph: Armed with an M9 rocket launcher, a bazooka-man
from the 29th Infantry Division runs by a burning Jagdpanzer 38, probably
from 2./PzJgAbt 246 (246. Volksgrenadier-Division) during fighting near
Aldenhoven during the third week of November 1944, part of the Operation
Queen offensive.

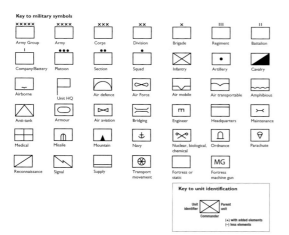

CONTENTS

INTRODUCTION

The rocket-propelled grenade launcher (RPG) has become a ubiquitous weapon on the modern battlefield; and all of these weapons trace their lineage back to the American 2.36in rocket launcher, better known as the bazooka. The bazooka was the serendipitous conjunction of two new technologies: the shaped-charge antitank warhead and the shoulder-fired rocket launcher. This book looks at the development of this iconic weapon, and traces its combat use on the World War II battlefield.

One of the widespread myths to have emerged about German tank design during World War II was the notion that German sideskirt armor was developed in response to the bazooka, and its British equivalent, the PIAT (Projector Infantry Antitank). American and British troops began encountering the new versions of German armored vehicles with extra armor shields in 1944, and so presumed that this new feature was in response to the Allied shaped-charge weapons. The shields received a variety of names including "bazooka shields," "bazooka pants," and "PIAT shields." In reality, their development was not a response to Allied shaped-charge weapons, for most German innovations in tank technology during the war years were prompted by developments on the Eastern Front.

This book examines the real story behind the bazooka shields. It also traces the many specialized devices developed by the Wehrmacht in World War II to deal with the threat of infantry close-attack weapons. A remarkable variety of curious devices was developed including a wood paste to defend against antitank charges, and a machine gun with a special curved barrel to allow armored vehicle crews to defend themselves from within the protective armor of their vehicle. As this book reveals, the bazooka was not the catalyst for these German efforts. The evolution of the Panzer after 1941 was much more strongly influenced by the battles against the Red Army on the Eastern Front. In the event, most experienced German tank

A dramatic scene, probably staged, as GIs rush a disabled Panther tank under the cover of a bazooka team in Normandy in late July 1944.

commanders were skeptical as to the value of these specialized devices and relied on the inherent capabilities of their tanks as well as prudent tactics to defend against the bazooka threat.

To examine the interplay of bazooka and Panzer, this book describes in detail one of the most intense skirmishes involving these two weapons – the battle for the twin villages of Krinkelt–Rocherath in Belgium on December 17–18, 1944 during the German Ardennes offensive. As this encounter demonstrates, the bazooka could be a very lethal weapon in the hands of a brave soldier, given the right circumstances. The battle also reveals the distinct limitations of these early antitank weapons.

A US soldier inspects a knocked-out PzKpfw IV Ausf J tank fitted with *Thoma-Schürzen*, the wire-mesh sideskirts developed to counter infantry antitank weapons.

CHRONOLOGY

1941

November 28 M10 grenade shaped-charge antitank rifle grenade adopted by US Army.

1942

March 5 Development of an antitank grenade projector approved.

April First prototypes of T1 rocket launcher assembled.

May 1 General Electric, Bridgeport, CT receives first T1 rocket launcher production contract.

June Experimental deployment of *S-Minenabwurfvorrichtung* on Eastern Front.

June 2 First batch of T1 launchers and rockets completed.

June 30 M1 rocket Launcher and M6 rocket recommended for standardization.

November 8 First combat use of M1 bazooka during Operation *Torch* landings in North Africa.

1943

January 28 Development of paratrooper rocket launcher approved.

February 25 Development of magneto trigger for rocket launcher approved.

August Application of *Zimmerit* anti-magnetic mine paste begins.

September 4 Production switches from M1 to M1A1 rocket launcher.

October 21 M9 rocket launcher recommended for standardization.

December *Maschinenpistolen Stopfen* firing ports deleted from German AFV production.

1944

March First *Nahverteidigungswaffe* fitted to German AFVs.

May Opening for *Rundumsfeuer* on StuG III production begins; few devices available.

July 20 M9A1 rocket launcher recommended to replace M1A1 launcher.

September 21 Polaroid T90 reflecting sight recommended for adoption.

October 26 Development of 3.5in rocket launcher recommended.

November 15 Authorization for use of *Kugellafette Vorsatz P* on Panzer IV/70(A).

December 16 Start of German Ardennes offensive.

December 17 Fighting for Krinkelt–Rocherath begins.

1945

January Production begins of *Kugellafette Vorsatz P*.

Sideskirt armor offered Panzers protection against small-caliber antitank rifles, but not larger antitank weapons. This StuG III assault gun was knocked out by tank-gun fire during fighting against the 4th Armored Division near Bitburg, Germany on February 27, 1945. This particular vehicle is also fitted with the *Rundumsfeuer* remote weapon station on the roof, though the machine gun is missing.

An MP 44 assault rifle fitted in a dismounted *Vorsatz P* mount by Allied intelligence. This combination is missing the magazine, periscope, and special arm brace.

DESIGN AND DEVELOPMENT

THE 2.36in ROCKET LAUNCHER

The development of the 2.36in rocket launcher resulted from the serendipitous conjunction of two separate technologies – shaped-charge warheads and solid rocket propulsion.

THE SHAPED CHARGE

The concept of shaped-charge explosives was developed independently in several countries. In the United States, it was discovered in the 1880s by Charles E. Munroe, a chemist with the US Navy Torpedo Station in Rhode Island. By detonating sticks of dynamite around a hollow tin can, Munroe found that the blast was enhanced in the direction of the hollow cavity, considerably increasing the destructive force in that direction. In Europe, the principle was more often called the Neumann Effect after similar experiments by Egon Neumann in Germany in 1910. A distinction is sometimes made between hollow charges and shaped charges. Hollow charges are explosive charges with a hollow cavity at the end opposite the initiation device. A shaped charge is a hollow charge, but with a metal liner on the inner face of the cavity.

It took decades before the Munroe or Neumann principle was linked to a weapon design to penetrate armor plate. In 1939, American and British liaison officers stationed

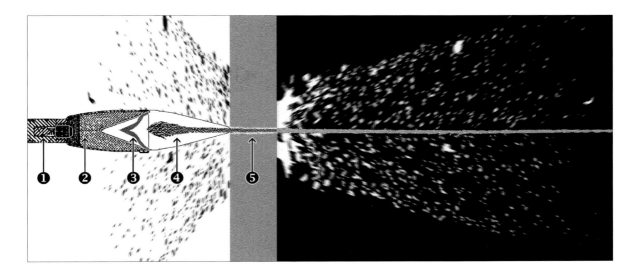

in Switzerland heard claims from the Swiss engineer Henri Mohaupt that he had developed a new type of explosive that had up to 40 times the destructive effect for an equal weight of explosive. A demonstration of his warhead to British officers seemed to back his claim, but Mohaupt was unwilling to explain the inner workings of his device unless paid an exorbitant fee. The British officers correctly surmised that the device worked on the Neumann principle and ended the negotiations. The Mohaupt warhead idea resurfaced in 1940 after he had come to an agreement with the Brandt ordnance firm in France over the development of an antitank rifle grenade. After the fall of France, the American agent for the Brandt firm persuaded the US Army Ordnance Department to examine the Mohaupt grenade. Mohaupt traveled to Aberdeen Proving Ground in Maryland and assembled about 200 grenades for trials. The tests were successful enough that negotiations began for the rights to the warhead design.

Curiously enough, Ordnance had earlier rejected a similar warhead design by Nevil M. Hopkins on the grounds that it was not a new invention, but covered by a 1911 patent. Once it was recognized that Mohaupt's invention was in fact a variation of the Munroe/Neumann effect, Ordnance renegotiated the rights to the Mohaupt concept at a considerably lower cost. The immediate outcome of the December 1940 trials was the design of the Special Rifle Grenade M9 that was adopted as standard in January 1941. This could penetrate 1.25in (32mm) of armor. The design was considered so secret, however, that no peacetime practice with the grenade was permitted, nor were any instruction manuals printed for troop use. The grenade was fired in the same fashion as other rifle grenades, i.e. from a special device placed on the end of the rifle's barrel and launched using a special blank cartridge.

It was quickly appreciated that the penetrative power of the M9 grenade would not be sufficient against newer tank armor, so the larger M10 grenade, which could penetrate 2in (50mm) of armor, was adopted on November 28, 1941. The M10 grenade was too large to fire from the usual rifle-grenade launcher, and the intention was to use it in conjunction with the .50-caliber heavy machine gun. Test launches resulted in considerable damage to the machine gun, however, and the concept was questioned since it had been hoped to deploy this grenade at platoon level or lower

This illustration shows the functioning of the bazooka's shaped-charge warhead. On impact, the spring-loaded fuze (**1**) is activated, detonating the shaped-charge warhead (**2**) which begins to deform and liquefy the metal liner (**3**) into a narrow plasma jet (**4**, **5**) with a temperature of about 36,000 degrees Fahrenheit (20,000 degrees Celsius), a velocity of 29,700ft/sec, and a density several times that of steel. The warhead detonation also creates a great deal of incandescent spall both outside and inside the tank, thus enhancing the warhead's destructive power.

where the .50-caliber machine gun was not available. Other weapons were tested including the British .55-caliber Boys antitank rifle and a new .60-caliber antitank rifle that was under development. As in the case of the machine-gun trials, these tests concluded that the recoil from the launch of the M10 grenade would damage the rifles. In February 1942, several solutions were examined including a dedicated launcher for the grenade, a special barrel to launch the grenade, and a launcher that could be mounted on an infantry rifle.

THE ROCKET ALTERNATIVE

Work on US Army rocket launchers can be traced back to World War I, when the rocket pioneer Robert Goddard demonstrated a "rocket gun" at Aberdeen Proving Ground shortly before the end of the war in 1918. Ordnance concluded that the weapon "could be developed to operate successfully against tanks," but the project was shelved after the war's end. One of Goddard's students, Clarence Hickman, continued his work and in 1942 was stationed at the US Navy's Indian Head Navy Firing Ground in Maryland, developing rocket propulsion for the National Defense Research Committee (NDRC). The US Army had a very modest rocket effort of its own, led by Leslie Skinner since 1933.

The conjunction of the warhead and rocket research was the result of the fortuitous insight of Gregory Kessenich of Ordnance's patent section, who realized that rocket propulsion might solve the problem of launching the M10 grenade. In August 1941, Kessenich brought this to the attention of Col Wiley Moore, chief of the Small Arms Division, who had been working on adapting the grenade to rifle launchers.

At the time, Maj Skinner and his assistant Lt Edward Uhl were working at Indian Head with Dr. Hickman on US Army rocket projects. The first step was to adapt a solid-propellant rocket motor to the grenade. Various spigot mortar options were studied including a simple launcher that clipped to the bayonet on an M1903 rifle. This was not especially accurate and M.C. Mogensen developed a special grenade launcher resembling a short rifle as a dedicated launcher for the grenade. This was not effective and Ordnance turned its attention to a cumbersome nine-round automatic launcher with three launch rails, each fed from a magazine above containing three rockets in three rows. Once again, the dispersion was too great. Eventually the Indian Head researchers realized that the problem was as much the granulation of the rocket propellant as the launchers themselves. The rocket propellant was reformulated for a faster burn time and the idea emerged to propel it out of a tube long enough that the rocket motor would have burned out before emerging from the tube,

A demonstration of the pilot T1 rocket launcher by one of its principal designers, Lt Edward Uhl, at Aberdeen Proving Ground in 1942. The tube was a simple length of steel tubing fitted with grip-stocks taken from .45-caliber Thompson submachine guns.

thereby protecting the gunner from the rocket blast. Tests of the rocket-propelled grenade revealed that the shroud fin used on the existing grenade did not offer stable flight, so this was replaced by blade fins.

Lt Uhl began designing a launcher using a corrugated tube, but this proved to be too fragile and difficult to manufacture. Uhl then found a 5ft length of pipe in the workshop scrap pile and this proved satisfactory. The pipe had two grip-stocks added to allow the gunner to aim the launcher, and an electrical trigger system was designed using an ordinary electric battery. Uhl demonstrated the launcher at Indian Head to Skinner and Hickman. In May 1942, Uhl demonstrated the launcher at Aberdeen Proving Ground to a senior delegation including BrigGen Gladeon Barnes, chief of the Ordnance technical staff, and LtGen Lesley McNair, commander of Army Ground Forces (AGF). The target was a moving M3 medium tank. Besides the new rocket launcher, the test also involved the various prototype spigot mortar designs. None of the spigot mortars managed to hit the tank, but Uhl struck it with his rocket launcher on his first attempt. McNair was so impressed with the demonstration that he asked Uhl if he could try firing the rocket launcher. After McNair launched a rocket, Barnes and several other officers followed suit,

The unsung hero of bazooka development was James L. Powers, an engineer at General Electric's Bridgeport, Connecticut plant where the weapon was eventually manufactured. Powers converted the Army's sketchy drawings into a practical design and was later involved in its gradual improvement. He had been responsible for the design of the Disposall kitchen garbage disposal, the plant's main product before the war, shown here in his right hand.

thus demonstrating the essential simplicity of the design. Barnes remarked that the launcher looked like the Bob Burns "bazooka," (the nickname given to a novelty musical instrument invented and used by the musical comedian Robin "Bob" Burns) and this name quickly stuck to the new weapon.

The next bazooka demonstration was held at Camp Simms near Washington, DC for a senior delegation including the US Army chief-of-staff LtGen George C. Marshall, accompanied by Allied liaison officers from Britain and the Soviet Union. Now called the T1 rocket launcher, the weapon so impressed Marshall that he ordered the immediate construction of 5,000 launchers and 25,000 rockets with speedy dispatch to forward-deployed Army units in Europe and the Pacific. Both the British and Soviet delegations also asked for shipments. Owing to its novelty, the T1 design was classified as secret, and the weapon was codenamed the Whip.

General Electric's Bridgeport, Connecticut plant had been manufacturing the M10 grenade so on May 1, 1942, it was awarded a production contract for 5,000 T1 launchers. No fewer than 14 different launchers were designed and tested along with numerous changes to the T1 rocket. The first batch of T1 launchers and rockets was completed on schedule on June 24, 1942, and both launcher and rocket were recommended for standardization as the M1 Antitank Rocket Launcher and M6 antitank rocket on June 30. Owing to British and Soviet interest in the weapon, a second order for 15,000 launchers quickly followed.

THE M1A1 ROCKET LAUNCHER

In reality, the bazooka was still not a mature weapon; and the M1 rocket launcher had gone into production before any prolonged testing had taken place. Pressure from senior army leaders led to its hasty introduction into service, but in June 1942 BrigGen Barnes recommended a delay in distribution to troops due to safety concerns. As a result, there was a continuing string of changes and amendments to the design in 1942–43.

During the spring of 1943, there were several accidents at Army bases in the southern United States when the rocket motor exploded, killing and injuring several soldiers. A study revealed that Ordnance had accepted a weaker steel for the tube than that of the prototypes to facilitate manufacture. Tubes made of this inferior steel were vulnerable to rupture on very hot days due to the higher pressure of the rocket motor. As a result, use of the bazooka in all locations except the combat zone was suspended in May 1943 and production of the M1 rocket launcher was halted temporarily on June 26, 1943. Two remedies were introduced. First, as a short-term expedient, Ordnance ordered the weight of the rocket propellant reduced. Second, the rear section of the launcher tube was wrapped with high-strength .05in steel wire. This also necessitated the redesign of the rocket wiring and contacts, since the wire wrap covered the area where the original electrical connector box and plunger had been located. In place of the brass ring on the rocket nose, a wire coil was stowed in the fins of the new rocket. The loader pulled the tab at the end of the wire and dragged it across a new contact clip fitted at the rear of the bazooka to complete the electrical firing circuit.

In cold weather, the rocket motor continued burning even after it had left the tube, injuring the face of the gunner. Reports about this from Tunisia led to a crash program commencing in late January 1943 to introduce a muzzle deflector. As a short-term solution, gunners were instructed to wear gloves and don a gas mask for protection. The deflector was accepted for production in April 1943 for retrofit to existing launchers, and this feature was incorporated on new-production launchers in November 1943. The deflector consisted of a conical wire-mesh screen that caught any large particles of rocket propellant debris, but which was open enough so as not to obscure the gunner's forward vision. (The NDRC eventually designed a new propellant called BBP (blastless bazooka propellant) that offered better propulsion as well as eliminating the high-temperature ruptures and low-temperature slow burns.) The trap at the rear of the rocket motor was also improved to prevent unburned rocket grain from congregating and contributing to ruptures. The improved rocket with the new ignition system and rocket motor was designated as the M6A1 2.36in rocket. The Army also issued simple face masks for bazooka gunners. These do not seem to have been widely used since the technical corrections to the launcher and rocket largely remedied the problems by 1944.

The changes to the launcher were extensive enough that the new launchers were designated as M1A1 when production started in September 1943. Besides the new-production launchers, Ordnance placed an order with General Electric to manufacture upgrade kits to retrofit the existing M1 launchers to the new M1A1 standards, and these were completed in July and early August 1943. In addition, kits were manufactured to modify older M6 rockets to the new ignition system necessary on the modified launchers. These were informally designated as M6A2 rockets in the

Problems with the early M1 rocket launcher in 1943 led to an Ordnance Field Services program to modify them to the M1A1 configuration at special overseas depots such as this one on Sicily in 1943. As can be seen, the rear of the tube is being wrapped with special steel wire for greater strength.

Mediterranean Theater of Operations. Special teams from the Ordnance Field Services were dispatched to the Mediterranean, European, and Pacific theaters to set up depots for modifying the existing launchers and rockets. A total of 59,932 M1A1 rocket launchers were manufactured through February 1944.

To deal with the recurrent problem of back-blast injuries to the gunner, the M1A1 introduced a muzzle deflector at the front of the launch tube. The deflector was made from wire mesh fine enough to catch errant propellant particles yet sufficiently transparent to allow the gunner to aim.

13

THE M9 ROCKET LAUNCHER

In November 1942, the Airborne Command made a formal request to Ordnance to develop a version of the bazooka that could be disassembled into two sections to make it easier to carry on parachute jumps. The main technical challenge was the design of a robust coupling to join the two sections of launch tube. The T21 launcher was ready for testing in February 1943, by which time there had been a string of complaints from the Mediterranean and Pacific theaters regarding the short life of ignition batteries, a general shortage of batteries, and the malfunction of the electrical system in wet weather. Ordnance decided to replace the troublesome battery ignition system with a magneto trigger, the Magnavox T6 electric firing mechanism, resulting in the T21E1 launcher. After test launchers were sent off to the service boards in June 1943 for further evaluation, Ordnance decided to incorporate the same wire wrapping on the rear section as had been developed for the M1A1 launcher, resulting in the T21E2 launcher. A small number of changes were recommended by the service boards and the new design was judged to be sufficiently superior that it should be adopted in place of the M1A1 launcher. The Infantry Board was not enthused about the two-part construction, however, fearing that it would lead to damage in the field; but the new ignition system and the improved gas deflector proved to be sufficient improvements to warrant Infantry Board acquiescence. The T21E2 was accepted as standard as the M9 2.36in rocket launcher on October 21, 1943 and production took place at General Electric from February through July 1944 in place of the M1A1.

The M9 rocket launcher was well regarded, not only for its anti-armor capabilities, but as a general-purpose infantry weapon for use against enemy bunkers and fortified positions. As a result, the Ordnance Committee decided that not only would the M9A1 replace the M9 in production, but that enough would be manufactured to

The M9 bazooka could be disassembled into two sections to make it easier to carry, as shown in this comparison of the M9 (right) and M1A1 (left) carried by two GIs of the 47th Infantry Regiment (9th Infantry Division) near Wollseiffen, Germany on February 16, 1945.

2.36in ROCKET LAUNCHERS

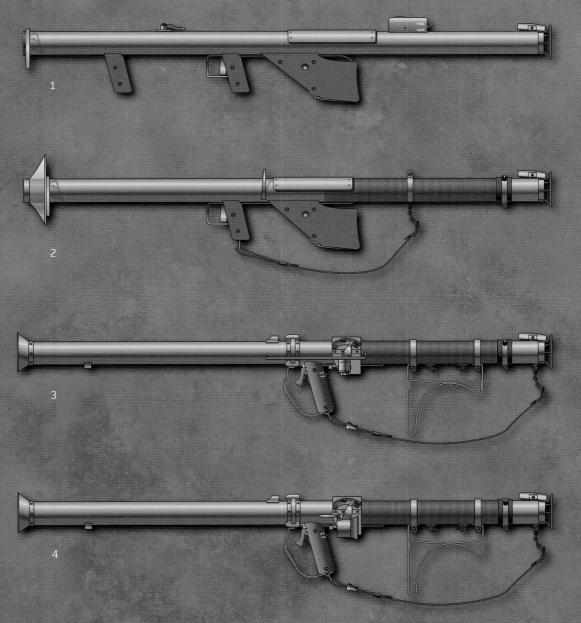

Type	M1 (1)	M1A1 (2)	M9 (3)	M9A1 (4)
Length	54in	54.7in	55.3in	55.3in
Ignition	battery	battery	magneto	magneto
Internal diameter	2.365in	2.365in	2.365in	2.365in
Weight	13lb	13.3lb	14.7lb	14.7lb
Maximum range	700yd	700yd	700yd	700yd
Effective range	300yd	300yd	300yd	300yd

The bazooka team of Cpl Bernie Heck and Pfc Virgil Thompson of D/376th Infantry (94th Infantry Division) were credited with knocking out four PzKpfw IV medium tanks during the attack by 11. Panzer-Division at Tettingen-Butzdorf on January 18, 1945. This is an M9A1 rocket launcher with the early General Electric T43 bar sight.

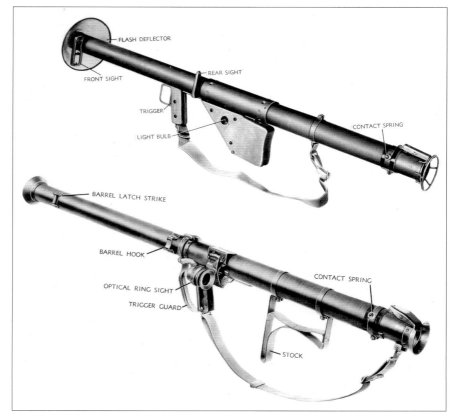

A comparison of first- and second-generation bazookas: the top launcher is a standard M1A1, while the bottom is an M18. The M18 was essentially similar to the late-production M9A1 launcher, but using an aluminum rather than steel tube. Development of the M18 was completed but it was not accepted for production due to the end of World War II.

completely replace the existing inventory of M1 and M1A1 bazookas in the field – a requirement that necessitated the addition of a second production facility. The Cheney Bigelow Wire Works in Springfield, Massachusetts was selected, beginning production September 1944. A total of 198,799 M9A1 launchers were manufactured by the two firms through May 1945 when further production was canceled in anticipation of newer types of rocket launcher.

THE M9A1 ROCKET LAUNCHER

Shortly after the first M9 bazookas were issued, it became apparent that the coupling between both sections could be distorted if dropped from shoulder height, as feared by the Infantry Board. A modified coupling was tested on the pilot M9E1 and once this performed satisfactorily in tests it was recommended for standardization as the M9A1 on April 8, 1944 and entered production in July 1944. This became the most widely produced version of the bazooka.

Ordnance had intended to fit the improved Polaroid T90 reflective sight to the M9 launcher, but it was not ready in time. As a substitute, General Electric developed the simple T43 bar sight. The Polaroid reflective sight was tested by the Infantry Board in August 1944, and approved for use in September 1944 on all new-production M9A1 rocket launchers as well as a retrofit to older launchers in the combat theaters.

PANZER DEFENSE AGAINST CLOSE ATTACK

THE EARLY YEARS

During the first years of World War II, the Wehrmacht did not develop any specialized devices to deal with the threat of infantry close attack because the inherent armored protection of the tank combined with prudent tactics proved more than sufficient. The success of the Panzer divisions during the Blitzkrieg era of 1939–41 was largely due to the ability of tanks to overcome infantry defenses quickly. Most armies of the period put their faith in the ability of infantry antitank guns, one of the widespread misconceptions to emerge from the Spanish Civil War (1936–39) being that antitank guns would sweep the battlefield of tanks the way that machine guns had swept the battlefield of infantry and cavalry in World War I. Although typical antitank guns of the 1939–41 period were indeed capable of knocking out tanks, their lack of numbers meant that the average infantry division had too thin a defensive crust to resist any sizable tank attack.

The Polish Army was relatively well equipped with antitank weapons, each infantry regiment having an antitank company with nine 37mm Bofors antitank guns. The Bofors guns were supplemented with an excellent new antitank rifle, the 7.92mm wz. 35, approximately 60 of which were assigned per regiment. Polish doctrine envisioned each regiment holding less than 5km (3 miles) of front, which translated into an antitank density of two antitank guns and six antitank rifles per kilometer (0.6 miles). German doctrine envisioned a Panzer attack on a narrow front, however, so a couple of antitank guns and several antitank rifles had little chance of stopping dozens of Panzers. Of the 2,626 German tanks taking part in the Polish campaign, 217 were destroyed and 457 were knocked out but deemed repairable – about one quarter of the total force. Given the magnitude and speed of the German victory, these losses were not regarded as unduly heavy.

The French Army of 1940 was one of the few during this period to eschew the use of antitank rifles. Instead, infantry antitank defense rested on 12 25mm antitank guns per infantry regiment. As a result, French infantry antitank defenses were less dense than their Polish equivalent, with only about three antitank guns per kilometer (0.6 miles) of front. Under these circumstances, French infantry units were quickly overwhelmed by Panzer attacks, and tank panic was not an uncommon occurrence. German losses in the 1940 campaign were significant, including 847 tanks destroyed of the 2,659 committed, with the losses falling most heavily on the lightly armored PzKpfw I and PzKpfw II. The better tanks such as the PzKpfw III and PzKpfw IV had 30mm frontal armor at this time while the light tanks had thinner armor, often only 15–20mm frontal armor. Nevertheless, the enormity of the German victories during the 1939–40 campaigns meant there was no particular urgency to upgrade Panzer armor protection; but efforts began to increase the frontal armor of medium tanks from 30mm to 50mm to deal with the better antitank guns in the 25mm–47mm range.

The Red Army of 1941 paralleled the French practice and relied on antitank guns for infantry defense. The 1941 rifle brigade had an antitank battalion with 12 45mm antitank guns, giving it roughly the equivalent defensive density as that of the French regiment of 1940. The official tables of organization also allocated each brigade an antitank-rifle company with 48 PTR-39 14.5mm antitank rifles. For a variety of reasons, none of these rifles were available at the time of the German attack in 1941.

The startling success of German Panzer attacks in June and July 1941 created a panic in Moscow, with calls for a crash program to deploy antitank rifles. Two 14.5mm rifles – the Degtyaryev PTRD and the Simonov PTRS – were put into serial production. The PTRD first went into combat use on the approaches to Moscow in October 1941, but it took some time for sufficient numbers of Soviet antitank rifles to become available. In the interim, the Red Army was forced to improvise with a host of expedients such as Molotov cocktails, hand-grenades, and simple rifle grenades – weapons of desperation that had a very low probability of damaging or destroying a tank. By the winter of 1941/42, however, the Soviet antitank rifles were beginning to have an impact. On February 18, 1942, the head of the German general staff, Generaloberst Franz Halder, complained to Minister of Armaments and War Production Albert Speer that the new Soviet antitank rifles were proving far more effective than the German 7.92mm PzB rifle; and he demanded that Speer take action.

SCHÜRZEN

By the spring of 1942, new versions of the PzKpfw III and PzKpfw IV medium tanks were appearing with 50mm frontal armor, based on the lessons of the 1940 campaign. This new armor level was proof against the Soviet antitank rifles at normal combat ranges. Even though the effectiveness of the rifles was decreasing due to frontal armor improvements, they were still capable of penetrating the side armor of most German tanks; and they remained a viable weapon due to the sheer numbers in use. At the beginning of 1942, there were only 8,116 antitank rifles in Red Army front-line service; by July 1942 the number had risen to 65,365 and by January 1, 1943 to

118,563. The growing numbers of antitank rifles allowed the Red Army to increase the density of antitank weapons per infantry regiment, from 27 in December 1941 to 54 per regiment by the summer of 1942. Authorized strength in the rifle division was 89 antitank rifles per division in December 1941, rising to 279 by March 1942. During the fighting on the approaches to Stalingrad in the summer and autumn of 1942, the Red Army began deploying special antitank battalions with 108 antitank rifles each.

In spite of the modest armor penetration capabilities of the Red Army's antitank rifles, their presence on the battlefield helped stifle the tank panic that had gripped many Soviet infantry units in the summer of 1941. Instead of being helpless against German tanks, the Soviet riflemen knew that they had a weapon that stood some chance of stopping a German tank. There is very little statistical data regarding the actual number of tank kills credited to the Soviet antitank rifles, however. The number of tanks actually destroyed was probably low, but the number of tanks damaged as well as crewmen killed or wounded was more significant.

By the end of 1942, the proliferation of Soviet antitank rifles had become a sufficiently serious problem that at the Führer conference of February 17, 1943, members of the Panzerkommission proposed to Hitler that a *Schutzpanzer* (armor shield) be added to German tanks. Daimler-Benz had developed a simple package of 5mm skirts for tank turrets and 10mm skirts for the hull sides. There were two options for the *Schürzen* (aprons): either soft-steel plates (*Platten*) or mesh screen (*Drahtgeflecht*). Samples of both types were tested at the Kummersdorf range on February 20, 1943; both types proved effective against captured Soviet antitank rifles, even at a minimal range of 100m (330ft). Aside from slowing the bullet as it passed through the screen, the impact often made the bullet unstable, which degraded penetration when the bullet finally came into contact with the main armor of the tank. Of the two types, the army selected the simple plate armor because a suitable mounting system was ready for use. In addition, there was some concern that it would take time to ramp up sufficient production capacity for the mesh screen. Hitler was given a demonstration in late March 1943, and ordered production of the plate armor.

Schürzen armor-plate aprons were first widely deployed during the Kursk campaign in the summer of 1943, as in the case of this PzKpfw IV Ausf H of 20. Panzer-Division. The *Schürzen* changed the silhouette of the PzKpfw IV, leading to its frequent misidentification as a Tiger tank by Soviet, American, and British opponents.

A detailed close-up from a wartime Allied intelligence report showing the wire mesh used for the *Thoma-Schürzen* (Thoma aprons).

Schürzen armor-plate aprons were added to new-production PzKpfw III and PzKpfw IV tanks as well as to StuG III assault guns by May 1943. The Tiger I heavy tank did not need such protection due to the fact that its thick side armor was already proof against antitank rifles. The new Panther received a modest set of skirts over its suspension as its upper hull and turret armor was proof against the Soviet antitank rifles.

THOMA-SCHÜRZEN AND RESILIENT APRONS

One of the problems with the side-armor aprons on German armored vehicles was that they tended to trap dust and road debris in the suspension cavity; and in mid-1944, the Wehrmacht decided it was time to switch to the wire-mesh aprons that had originally been tested in 1942. Further work on these aprons was overseen in 1943 by Oberst Wolfgang Thomale, chief-of-staff of the office of the Generalinspekteur der Panzertruppen (Inspector General of the Panzer Troops). The final configuration of wire mesh selected for production was woven from 5mm (0.2in) steel wire spaced about 15mm (0.6in) apart. Aside from solving the dust problem, these aprons were about 600kg (1,320lb) lighter than the steel plate types. The turret aprons remained of the sheet type. The new aprons were intended for the new PzKpfw IV Ausf J and related types such as the Panzer IV/70(A). First introduced in September 1944, the wire-mesh aprons were nicknamed *Thoma-Schürzen* (Thoma aprons).

PzKpfw IV Ausf J SPECIFICATIONS

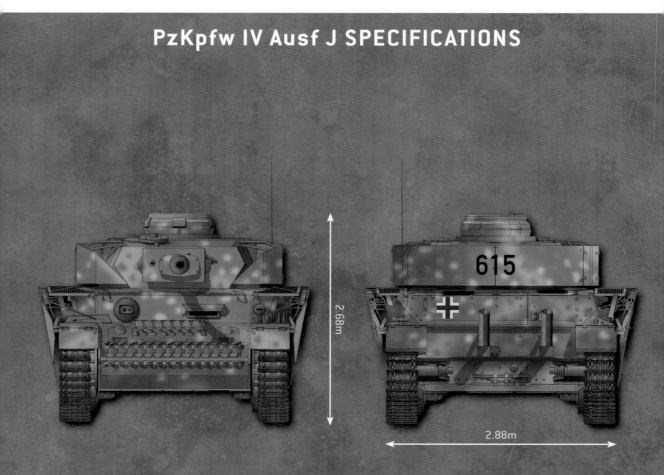

615

2.68m

2.88m

6./SS-PzRgt 12, DECEMBER 1944

Crew: 5
Weight: 25 metric tonnes (27.6 short tons)
Length: 7.02m (22ft 10in)
Width: 2.88m (9ft 4in)
Height: 2.68m (8ft 8in)
Main armament: 7.5cm KwK 40
Secondary armament: Two 7.92mm MG 34

Engine: Maybach HL 120 TRM112
Maximum speed: 38km/h (23mph)
Road range: 320km (192 miles)
Turret front armor: 50mm (2in)
Turret side armor: 30mm (1.2in)
Hull front armor: 80mm (3.2in)
Hull side armor: 30mm (1.2in)

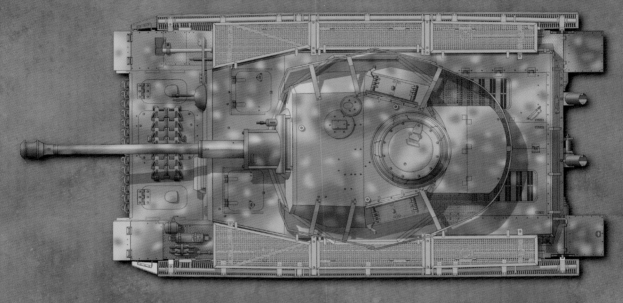

7.02m

DEFENDING AGAINST CHIMERAS

Although the skirt armor was developed to protect German tanks against a specific threat, other German innovations stemmed from their own experiences while attempting to defeat Soviet tanks. One of the most curious cases was *Zimmerit*, an anti-magnetic mine coating that appeared on German armored vehicles in 1943–44. German engineers presumed that because German magnetic antitank weapons had proved so effective, the Red Army would follow suit with their own magnetic antitank weapons, hence the development of *Zimmerit*.

The German infantry faced its own tank panic in 1941 with the appearance of the heavily armored Soviet T-34 medium tank and the KV heavy tank. German 37mm antitank guns were ineffective against these new tanks, and the new 50mm guns were only marginally better. German antitank rifles were completely ineffective and were abandoned much earlier than in the Red Army. As in the Soviet case, a variety of improvised means were developed to give the German infantry some chance of knocking out Soviet tanks. Such improvisations included grenade bundles, and rifle grenades with shaped-charge warheads, but these were mainly weapons of desperation with a very low probability of killing a Soviet tank. The most effective German close-attack weapons were the various shaped-charge antitank munitions. One such was the Hafthohlladung 3 HL (adhesive hollow charge) hand-emplaced shaped charge that employed magnets to attach it against a tank. Developed by the Wehrmacht, this close-attack weapon became available in the autumn of 1942. The 3kg (6.6lb) device had a powerful 150mm shaped charge with a theoretical penetration of 140mm (5.6in) of armor – more than enough to deal with any Soviet tank of the era. About 8,500 of these were manufactured in late 1942, and more than 358,400 in 1943.

The use of these various infantry antitank devices required a great deal of courage on the part of the soldier. The Wehrmacht encouraged such gallantry with the establishment on March 9, 1942 of the *Sonderabzeichen für das Niederkämpfen von Panzerkampfwagen durch Einzelkämpfer* (Special Award for Close Attack of Tanks by Individual Fighters), better known as the *Panzerknacker* award. This was issued in two levels, for the destruction of one or five enemy tanks. German records suggest that over 18,500 of these awards were issued, mainly on the Eastern Front, accounting for over 20,650 enemy tanks and armored vehicles. Many if not most of these awards came in the later years of the war, when German antitank rockets such as the *Panzerschreck* and *Panzerfaust* became available.

The success of the Hafthohlladung 3 HL prompted the Panzerkommission (working on the presumption that the Red Army would copy its simple design) to recommend that German tanks be protected against a Soviet version of a magnetic close-attack weapon. Development of an anti-magnetic coating began in late 1942 and was essentially a wood putty. The coating was called *Zimmerit*, after the name of its developer and manufacturer, the Berlin paint company Chemische Werke Zimmer. The principal ingredients were Mowilith 20 (polyvinyl acetate glue) mixed with sawdust, plus various anti-corrosive paint additives and coloring. The *Zimmerit* paste was only applied to vertical surfaces since it would have no value on horizontal surfaces. An initial layer of *Zimmerit* was applied to prime the surface. Once dry, a second layer was applied with a notched trowel to create a corrugated finish. This

A close-up of the bow of a Panzer IV/70(V) showing the coating of *Zimmerit* paste. This captured vehicle was subjected to bazooka trials by the First US Army near Aachen in December 1944, with the rocket impacts marked in chalk. The bazooka had marginal performance against the 80mm (3.2in)-thick frontal armor of this vehicle.

second textured surface reduced the chance that a magnetic mine or sticky mine would adhere to the tank. Once applied, the *Zimmerit* paste was dried using a blowtorch that evaporated the benzene solvent in the Mowilith 20 and hardened the coating. It is worth noting that the corrugated pattern varied from factory to factory, with many different styles evident on German vehicles.

Zimmerit application started in late August–early September 1943 and was applied to tanks, tank destroyers, and assault guns. It was used for about a year, and was abandoned on September 7, 1944 by order of the Generalinspekteur der Panzertruppen, Generaloberst Heinz Guderian. There have been various explanations for its abandonment. Some sources suggest that there were reports that *Zimmerit* could be ignited when hit with various type of incendiary projectiles. The Soviet magnetic-mine threat never emerged, however, and this was probably a contributing factor in its demise.

NAHVERTEIDIGUNGSWAFFE: THE CLOSE DEFENSE WEAPON

The development of a specialized weapon to defend against close infantry attack did not take place until 1943. This weapon did not have a particularly high priority, and indeed its development had more to do with other aspects of German tank design. It was intended to replace three different tank devices: the *Nebelkerzen Wurfgerät* smoke launcher, *Minenabwurfvorrichtung* mine discharger, and *Maschinenpistolen Stopfen* pistol ports.

German tanks had been fit with the *Nebelkerzen Abwurfvorrichtung* (smoke device fitting) since 1938. This was a smoke-candle rack, fitted at the rear of the tank above the muffler. The five *Schnellnebelkerzen* (fast smoke grenades) were ignited on the rack

The *Nebelkerzen Wurfgerät* smoke-launcher apparatus was usually fitted in clusters of three tubes, as evident on the front corner of the superstructure of this StuG III assault gun photographed in Italy during 1944. This photo also provides a good example of the *Schürzen* armor-plate aprons.

and discharged smoke for 100–200 seconds. The intention was for an attacking tank formation to ignite these devices on several tanks simultaneously to obscure the larger formation from enemy antitank guns; it was not useful for shielding an individual tank except during retreat. These devices were officially abandoned in April 1942 because they had not proven to be very effective.

In their place, the Nebelkerzen Wurfgerät 1 (smoke-grenade launcher) was developed and first experimentally mounted on the PzKpfw III Ausf L in March 1942. It was officially adopted on new-production tanks and assault guns in September 1942. Each tank had a cluster of three launch tubes on both sides of the turret. The Schnellnebelkerze 39 smoke grenades were ejected in front of the tank using a small charge screwed to the base of a smoke candle that was triggered electrically. The six tubes could be activated individually from a small control panel inside the turret, or launched simultaneously. Although the system worked better than the earlier *Nebelkerzen Abwurfvorrichtung*, there were reports in February 1943 that enemy small-arms and artillery fire was igniting the smoke grenades while still in their tubes, thus incapacitating the crew. Tank crews were instructed to stop loading the smoke candles into the launchers, and in June 1943, the device was formally withdrawn from production on new tanks and assault guns.

The first dedicated weapon to defend against close attack was the *Minenabwurfvorrichtung* mine discharger. This was a very simple device consisting of a small steel tube oriented at a 50-degree angle and bolted to the hull or track guards of the tank. The tube contained a special Panzer version of the S-Mine (Schutzenmine 35), better known to Allied troops as the "Bouncing Betty." The first examples of this device were sent for troop trials on PzKpfw III Ausf Ls with various units on the Eastern Front in June 1942. They were subsequently adopted as standard equipment on new-production Tiger I tanks from January through October 1943; but it is not clear why

they were not more widely employed for tank defense aside from on the Tiger I. They certainly would have been vulnerable to unintentional detonation from enemy fire, as was the case with the smoke-candle launchers. In addition, unintentional launch near friendly infantry would no doubt have been a concern. In the event, they were abandoned in the autumn of 1943 after only a few hundred Tiger Is had been fitted with them.

Until late 1943, many German tanks and assault guns were fitted with *Maschinenpistolen Stopfen*. These were simple firing ports that permitted the crew to use their MP 38 or MP 40 submachine guns to fire at enemy infantry. These pistol ports were not especially efficient since it was hard to aim weapons through them; furthermore, they compromised the integrity of the tank's armor. In December 1943, *Maschinenpistolen Stopfen* were dropped from German armored vehicles on the production lines in favor of a new *Nahverteidigungswaffe* (close-defense weapon). This new device was intended to replace the smoke dischargers, mine launchers, and pistol ports.

The *Nahverteidigungswaffe* close-defense weapon was a simple, breech-loaded mortar tube, inclined at 50 degrees and fitted in a traversable mounting on the turret or casemate roof. In its most elementary form, it was used to eject the standard 92mm Schnellnebelkerze 39 smoke grenades. Unlike the externally mounted launchers, however, the smoke grenade was not exposed to hostile fire, being loaded into the launcher from within the vehicle through a simple hinged breech and launched by triggering the ejection charge at their base. Besides its use to launch smoke candles, the *Nahverteidigungswaffe* was designed to mate with a standard 26mm *Kampfpistole* (combat pistol).

The *Minenabwurfvorrichtung* mine discharger was a simple inclined tube used to launch S-Minen. It can be seen here on the left side of this Tiger I heavy tank, above the rampaging bull insignia of sPzAbt 505. In this case, during the battle of Kursk, it is not fit with an S-Mine. These devices posed a hazard to nearby infantry or crew if the mine was detonated by enemy small-arms or artillery fire.

A *Nahverteidigungswaffe* close-defense weapon is shown here toward the top of the photo, fitted to the upper-right corner of the roof of a Panther Ausf G tank.

THE *RUNDUMSFEUER*

Although German tanks were well provided with self-defense weapons, assault guns such as the StuG III were not. The StuG III was issued a single MG 34 or MG 42 machine gun, and this was operated by the loader from behind a simple armored shield on the roof of the vehicle. As a result, the loader was very exposed when trying to defend the assault gun, especially in the event of infantry close attack. The solution to this was the development of a remote-control weapon station, called the *Rundumsfeuer*. This was mounted in the same location on the right-side roof of the StuG III, but the loader could fire the weapon from within the protective armor of the vehicle through the use of a periscopic sight. This weapon system was also adopted on the next-generation assault gun, the Jagdpanzer 38 (Hetzer), which – contrary to its name – was deployed as an assault gun and not as a tank destroyer. The *Rundumsfeuer* was also considered as the auxiliary armament for the newer *Jagdpanzer* tank destroyer, the Jagdpanzer IV. Although it was test-fitted to the prototypes, the intended standoff role of these vehicles reduced the perceived need for such a weapon – at least at first.

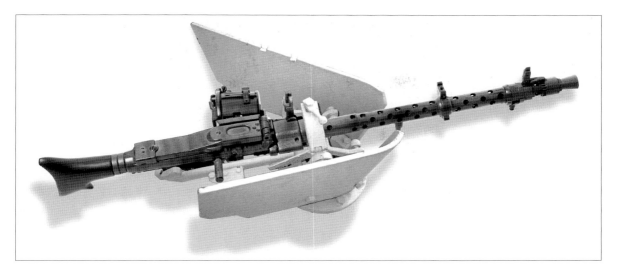

THE *VORSATZ P*

When some of the later production run of the Jagdpanzer IV began to be issued as expedient tanks to normal Panzer units, the auxiliary armament issue was reconsidered. Instead of the use of the *Rundumsfeuer*, a less expensive but more exotic weapon system was adopted: the *Kugellafette Vorsatz P* (Panzer-type ball-mounting). This roof mounting enabled the crew to defend their vehicle from inside using an MP 44 assault rifle. What was unusual about the device was that it employed a curved barrel to enable the crew to spray gunfire around the vehicle. The development of this weapon was another case of technological serendipity.

The Rheinmetall-Borsig plant at Guben was responsible for testing automatic cannon and constructed a large-caliber curved barrel as a means to deflect the projectiles

An illustration showing the details of a *Rundumsfeuer* remote-control weapon station from overhead, fitted with an MG 34 machine gun.

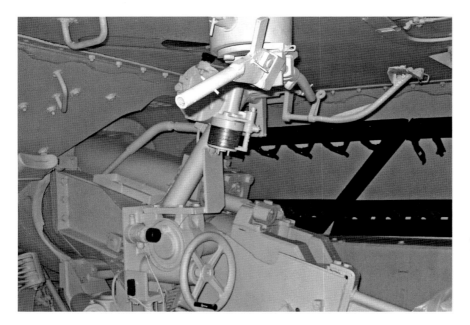

A detail view of the interior portion of the *Rundumsfeuer*, in a restored Jagdpanzer 38 (Hetzer) at the US Army Ordnance Museum, Aberdeen Proving Ground.

A close-up of the *Vorsatz P* ball-mounting viewed from the side, showing the 90-degree curve. The ball-mounting absorbed much of the energy from the bullet impact against the curved barrel.

during testing rather than firing them to full range. The engineers were surprised that the curved deflector suffered so little damage. Oberst Hans Schaede, who headed a research lab at the Rheinmetall-Borsig facility in Sömmerda, wondered whether a curved barrel (*Krummerlauf*) could be built that would allow infantry to fire from the protection of their trenches or for armored-vehicle crews to defend their vehicle. Trials in 1944 concluded that an infantry weapon using a 30-degree curve was feasible, but that any greater a curvature made the weapon uncontrollable. On the other hand, a vehicle version could be fitted in an armored mount that would absorb much of the shock, and so a 90-degree barrel was developed. The MP 44 assault rifle was the preferred weapon for this device since its ammunition was not as powerful as ordinary Gew 98 rifle ammunition, and it offered fully automatic fire. Schaede was awarded the Knight's Cross of the War Merit Cross in November 1944 for his discoveries.

Final design of the weapon was undertaken by Dr. Richard Braun at Rheinmetall-Borsig's proving ground at Unterlüß. A prototype of the weapon was fitted to a prototype of the Panzer IV/70(A) and demonstrated to Hitler on July 6, 1944. The initial priority was given to the armored vehicle mount, the *Kugellafette Vorsatz P*, rather than to the *Vorsatz I* infantry mount. Production was assigned to the main Düsseldorf/ Derendorf plant with plans to manufacture 20,000 devices per month; but this plant was severely damaged by US bombers during a raid on September 9, 1944, thus delaying production until after the Ardennes battles described in this book. The Waffenamt authorized the issue of *Vorsatz P* for the Panzer IV/70(A) on November 15, 1944, though none was ready at this point. The first batch of about 1,500 curved-barrel kits were manufactured in January 1945; production collapsed shortly afterward. The Panzer IV/70(A) was a version of the PzKpfw IV tank with a fixed casemate and the longer 7.5cm gun of the Panther tank. Although originally conceived as *Panzerjäger*, these vehicles were issued as expedient tanks to normal Panzer units. In January 1945, they were also issued to some *Sturmgeschütz* brigades as a means to provide them with some long-range firepower. Owing to their original *Panzerjäger* role, they lacked the usual coaxial machine gun and hull machine-gun mount of normal tanks. For self-defense, they had just a single socket-mount on the right front of the superstructure for use in conjunction with an MG 42 machine gun; and the lack of adequate means of self-defense was one of the main reasons these vehicles

received priority for the *Vorsatz P* self-defense machine-gun mount. These mounts were issued so late in the war that there are few if any accounts of their use, but photographic evidence does prove that they were issued to combat units.

A Panzer IV/70(A) knocked out during the fighting against the 745th Tank Battalion and 78th Infantry Division near Uckerath on March 28, 1945. This illustration provides a clear view of the *Thoma-Schürzen*. A close inspection of the roof hatches also reveals the fitting for the *Vorsatz P* self-defense weapon.

Besides the *Vorsatz P* mount for AFVs, the *Vorsatz I* (infantry mount) was also developed to enable German infantrymen to fire from the security of a trench. The barrel on this version was not as sharply curved, and it was fitted with a special reflective sight.

TECHNICAL SPECIFICATIONS

THE BAZOOKA ASSESSED

FIRING PROCEDURE

The bazooka was served by a two-man crew: gunner and loader. The loader inserted the rocket into the rear end of the launch tube. Once the warhead section was in the tube, the loader carefully removed a safety pin located in the middle of the rocket that prevented the impact fuze from detonating the warhead. The loader then pushed the rocket all the way into the tube which completed the electrical firing circuit when a brass ring on the rocket nose came in contact with a spring-loaded electrical contact above the tube, and a contact on the rocket fin came in contact with a tail latch at the rear of the launcher. The standard procedure was for the loader to tap the gunner on the helmet to indicate that the launcher was loaded. Loaders were instructed to move away from the rear of the bazooka as quickly as possible since the exhaust gas from the rocket when fired was dangerous.

The gunner aimed the bazooka using a simple blade sight along with a front sight near the muzzle that had horizontal steps gradated at ranges of 100yd, 200yd, 300yd, and 400yd. The first 5,237 launchers had ambidextrous sights that could be used by right- or left-handed gunners. The traversable sight above the tube proved too easy to damage, however, so the sights were welded in place on the left side and the right-side

range ladder was deleted, limiting the later bazookas to right-handed use. The sight was modified again at launcher 49,202 by pulling back the sight 2.5in from the muzzle, and a peep sight was welded to the tube in the hopes of encouraging the gunner to use binocular vision when aiming the weapon. At the same time, the 400yd range position was eliminated to simplify the sight since it was recognized that the bazooka was seldom accurate at that range.

The successful use of the bazooka in combat usually required a heroic gunner. The bazooka was not a dependable weapon, and as the accounts in this book demonstrate, it would often fail to fire or the warhead would fail to detonate properly. Effective use of the bazooka required both courage and persistence. The same was true of its German and British equivalents, the *Panzerschreck*, *Panzerfaust*, and PIAT. Even though the bazooka was effective at ranges of 300yd or more, the average range for a successful engagement of an enemy tank in World War II was only 55yd. At least 15 US soldiers were awarded the Medal of Honor for actions involving the bazooka; three of these were in the Pacific theater, one in Italy, and 11 in the European theater. Of those in the ETO, three would be awarded for actions during the Ardennes campaign.

The 2.36in bazooka rocket launcher was crewed by two men, the gunner and loader, as shown here during a training exercise with an M1 rocket launcher in Britain on May 28, 1943. The bazooka was a very simple weapon. Below the launch tube were two pistol grips, the aft one with a trigger. Behind these was a wooden shoulder stock containing two cavities with two B-cell batteries in each. One of the cavities was wired to ignite the rocket motor; the second cavity contained spare batteries. The shoulder stock also contained a small light used to test whether the battery still had enough charge to function properly.

IMPROVING THE ROCKETS

There were numerous complaints from the field that the bazooka rockets often failed to detonate. Part of the problem was the lack of training of the bazooka loaders – in the heat of battle, the loaders often forgot to remove the safety pin while loading the weapon, which meant that the impact fuze could not function. However, Ordnance tests revealed that the existing metal ogive (nose cone) tended to telescope on impact, cushioning the impact shock, and resulting in the failure of the impact fuze. In addition, the ogive tended to shear off from the rest of the body at impact angles of 20 degrees or more, causing poor warhead penetration even if the warhead detonated. The solution to this was the redesign of the ogive from a bullet shape to a simple rounded shape, with the resulting rocket designated as the M6A3. The new ogive and other improvements led to a reduction in the function time of the impact fuze from 1,250 microseconds on the M6A1 to only 875 microseconds on the M6A3 that improved armor penetration by offering a better standoff distance. In conjunction with various other improvements, the M6A3 warhead's maximum armor penetration increased from 3in (75mm) to 4in (100mm). The M6A3 also introduced a circular fin that improved the ballistic performance of the rocket compared to that of the M6A1. The M6A3 was introduced along with the M9 launcher, and could also be fired from the earlier M1A1 launcher.

The use of the bazooka as a general-purpose weapon led to interest in other types of warheads, resulting in a variety of smoke, incendiary, and high-explosive warheads being developed and tested. The only type to see widespread production was the M10 Smoke rocket. Featuring a WP (white phosphorus) fill, which gave it a secondary incendiary effect, the M10 Smoke rocket took the place of two separate rockets: the T31 thermite incendiary rocket and the T27E1 HC (hexachloroethane) smoke rocket. The M26 chemical-agent rocket with a CK (phosgene) warhead was also accepted for service use, but not deployed. Besides the combat rockets, M7 training rockets with an inert warhead section were also manufactured.

A spectacular demonstration of the effect of a bazooka rocket on impact against an old M3 light tank at Camp Roberts, California, in 1944. The explosion of the shaped-charge warhead had significant secondary effects including incandescent spall both inside and outside the tank.

2.36in rocket production					
Type	1942	1943	1944	1945	Total
HEAT rockets	155,000	1,937,000	6,033,000	4,871,000	*12,996,000*
WP smoke rockets	0	8,000	1,389,000	1,210,000	*2,607,000*

2.36IN BAZOOKA ROCKETS

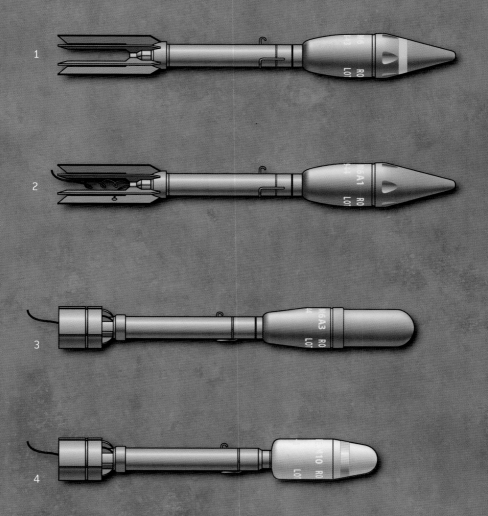

Type	M6 (1)	M6A1 (2)	M6A3 (3)	M10 (4)
Length	21.6in	21.6in	19.4in	17.1in
Weight	3.4lb	3.4lb	3.4lb	3.4lb
Muzzle velocity	265ft/sec	265ft/sec	265ft/sec	265ft/sec
Warhead type	HEAT	HEAT	HEAT	Smoke
Warhead fill	Pentolite	Pentolite	Pentolite	White phosphorus
Warhead fill weight	0.5lb	0.5lb	0.5lb	0.9lb
Armor penetration	3in/75mm	3in/75mm	4in/100mm	n/a
Fuze	Impact	Impact	Impact	Impact

PANZER DEFENSES ASSESSED

EASTERN FRONT LESSONS

The *Schürzen* aprons first saw widespread combat use in the summer of 1943 at Kursk; and they proved to be quite effective. A StuG III gunner, Armin Sohns, described his experiences during the fighting south of Kremenchug on the Dnepr River in October 1943:

> Our vehicle received no less than ten hits by A/T rifles on the left side apron. Seven of these, hitting at an angle, glanced off, leaving dents just short of penetrations. Three were clean penetrations, but not enough punch left to do damage to the vehicle. We were unaware of these hits until we examined out StuG after the action. The problem was these A/T rifles offered a very small target not much bigger than an ordinary rifleman, and were almost impossible to detect. (Sohns 1968: 9)

The propaganda service of the Wehrmacht gave a great deal of publicity to the valiant *Panzerknacker*, which attracted the interest of the highest levels of the German armed forces to the potential threat of enemy close attack against the Panzers. Some senior leaders thought that tanks would soon be obsolete and ineffective due to the advent of new handheld antitank weapons such as the bazooka and *Panzerfaust*. This opinion was not shared by the leadership of the Panzer force, however, who recognized the limitations of these new antitank weapons.

Data from the office of the Generalinspekteur der Panzertruppen provided the evidence. In January 1944, German kill claims against Soviet tanks were 3,670, of which only 114 (3.1 percent) were attributed to infantry close-combat weapons, mainly of the *Panzerfaust* or *Panzerschreck* types; for February 1944 the tank kill claims were 1,219, of which only 62 (5 percent) were attributed to infantry weapons. Soviet figures in records for the same period from the 1st Belorussian Front are similar, indicating that only 3 percent of tank losses were due to German infantry close-attack weapons. German tank commanders attributed the limited success of these weapons to their short range. Panzer tactics stressed the need to suppress enemy infantry with machine-gun and cannon fire from distances beyond the effective range of the new rocket weapons.

TESTING THE *THOMA-SCHÜRZEN*

When the wire-mesh aprons were first widely encountered by the US Army in the Ardennes in December 1944–January 1945, Allied commentators presumed that they were intended to defend against the bazooka. Some US armored officers decided to test them as a possible antidote to the German bazooka analogs such as the *Panzerfaust* and *Panzerschreck*. As a result of these tests, it quickly became apparent that the aprons had no effect at all in stopping the penetration of the bazooka or similar antitank weapons.

A similar controversy embroiled the Wehrmacht around the same time when, in December 1944, the 4. Panzerarmee Waffenschule (weapons school) on the Eastern Front reported that wire-mesh aprons as well as *elastische Schürzen* ("resilient aprons") could degrade the effectiveness of *Panzerfaust* and *Panzerschreck* projectiles. The Soviets had captured large quantities of *Panzerfaust* rockets, and now Red Army forces were

When the US Army first encountered the *Thoma-Schürzen* in December 1944–January 1945, it was widely presumed that they were intended to protect against bazooka attack. A team from the 1st Armored Group in the Sarrebourg area in Alsace decided to test this idea to establish whether the wire-mesh apron would provide protection against German shaped-charge rockets. Here, an officer shows how they plan to fire a 2.36in bazooka rocket against an improvised screen mimicking *Thoma-Schürzen* on a derelict PzKpfw IV.

As can be seen in this detail view, the *Thoma-Schürzen* had no effect on the bazooka detonation which still penetrated the side armor, as evidenced by the hole and the characteristic spall pattern around it. Traces of *Zimmerit* paste can be seen on the far right and on the parts of the turret face.

PANZER SELF-DEFENSE MUNITIONS

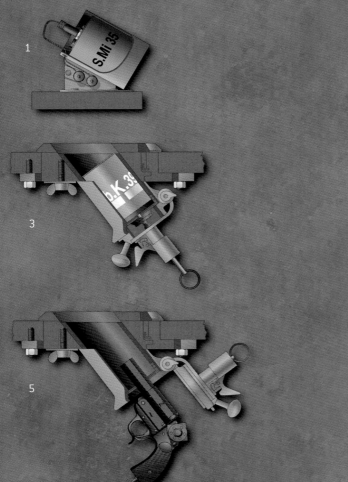

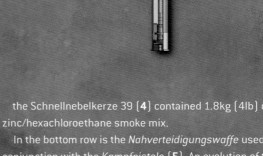

At top left is the *S-Minenabwurfvorrichtung* mine discharger with S-Mine loaded (**1**). Filled with 182g (6oz) of high explosive plus steel balls, measuring 130mm (5in) in length, and weighing 4kg (9lb), the S-Mine (**2**) differed from conventional anti-personnel mines. When it was activated by contact or a tripwire, it launched a munition into the air. This trailed a steel wire about 0.7m (27in) in length which detonated the mine, spraying the surrounding area with steel balls. The Panzer version of the S-Mine used an electrically activated Glühzünder 28 fuze that was triggered electrically from inside the tank using a small control panel.

In the middle row is the *Nahverteidigungswaffe* close-defense weapon with Schnellnebelkerze 39 smoke grenade fitted (**3**). Weighing 2kg (4.5lb) and 145mm (5.6in) long,

the Schnellnebelkerze 39 (**4**) contained 1.8kg (4lb) of a zinc/hexachloroethane smoke mix.

In the bottom row is the *Nahverteidigungswaffe* used in conjunction with the *Kampfpistole* (**5**). An evolution of the earlier smoothbore *Leuchtpistole* (flare pistol), the *Kampfpistole* (combat pistol) had a rifled barrel with a new family of rounds including high-explosive, smoke, and flares. Weighing 200g (7oz), 165mm (6.6in) long, and filled with 70g (2.5oz) of high explosive, the 326 Lp Pz Sprenggranatpatrone mit Zeitzünder (explosive round with time fuze; **6**) was a special round for tank defense developed for the *Kampfpistole*. After being ejected using a small charge, the round trailed a 300mm (12in) steel wire that detonated the munition about 0.5–2m (1ft 8in–6ft 6in) above the ground.

USING THE *VORSATZ P*

The muzzle of the MP 44 assault rifle was attached to the *Vorsatz P* ball-mount by means of an adapter. Since the MP 44 was oriented vertically when in use, it was impractical to use the usual shoulder stock. As a result, a special brace was clipped to the assault rifle. The operator used his right hand to pull the trigger and his left hand (in conjunction with the brace) to move the weapon. Aiming the MP 44 was made possible by a Zeiss Ziehlfurnrohr WZF 5811 periscopic sight mounted in the ball-mount parallel to the assault rifle, providing a 12-degree field of view at 1.25×. Rheinmetall tests concluded that the weapon offered an effective range of 600m (660yd) when fired in single-shot mode and 300m (330yd) when fired in full-automatic mode.

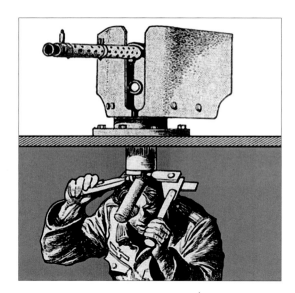

using them against German armored vehicles. As a result, the Waffenamt (Weapons Agency) instructed the *Panzerfaust* manufacturer, HASAG in Leipzig, to test the weapon against plate and mesh aprons as well as various types of fabric aprons made from burlap, as promoted by 4. Panzerarmee's weapons school. HASAG reported that tests on December 3, 1944 had shown that the aprons did not degrade the penetration of shaped-charge rockets. These tests were followed by similar tests at the Kummersdorf proving ground on December 21, 1944, using actual PzKpfw IV and captured M4 tanks fitted with various aprons and sandbags. Once again, the trials showed that the aprons did not diminish the performance of shaped-charge warheads.

What was not appreciated at the time was that shields actually enhanced the penetration of shaped-charge rockets such as the bazooka. One of the main shortcomings of the bazooka's warhead design was that there was too little time between impact and detonation for the ideal formation of the penetrating jet due to the slow activation speed of its simple impact fuze. Detonation of the bazooka warhead against a skirt provided more time for the fuze to trigger the warhead, allowing the jet to form more coherently, thus enhancing its penetrative effects. This did not become evident until after the war, when advances in flash radiography better documented this phenomenon.

A wartime Allied intelligence illustration showing how the vehicle crewman operated the *Rundumsfeuer*. A periscopic sight was fitted to the center of the mounting for observation and targeting, with the lens visible slightly below the machine-gun barrel.

EVALUATING THE CLOSE-COMBAT WEAPONS

The Panzer by its very nature was a formidable anti-infantry weapon, even without the later developments in anti-infantry technology. During the early years of World War II both the PzKpfw III and PzKpfw IV had a ball-mounted machine gun in the hull to defend against infantry, as well as a coaxial machine gun in the turret. In addition, their main guns were capable of firing a very potent high-explosive round that was intended primarily to deal with enemy infantry. For close defense, most German tanks of that era had small pistol ports that could be used in conjunction with the crew's self-defense weapons. Most tank crews also carried hand-grenades that could be thrown out the tank hatches to deal with any enemy infantry foolish enough to jump on the tank.

In reality, the *Nahverteidigungswaffe* would be used mainly for firing smoke grenades or flares. In spite of its name, it was not really very useful for close defense because it was difficult to aim with any accuracy and the 326 Lp Pz Sprenggranatpatrone mit Zeitzünder (explosive round with time fuze) was not really powerful enough to dissuade a determined enemy infantryman.

Allied intelligence personnel fired a few magazines of ammunition through the *Vorsatz P*. As can be seen here, many of the bullets were deformed and buckled when forced to curve.

THE COMBATANTS

TACTICAL DEVELOPMENTS

THE MEDITERRANEAN THEATER

The first bazookas to be deployed went to the British 8th Army in the Middle East, arriving in Egypt in September 1942. An Ordnance liaison officer, Col G.B. Jarrett, demonstrated the Whip. The British officers felt that the weapon was not suitable for desert use since the operator required concealment until the enemy tank was close enough to be engaged. As a result, the first batch of 600 launchers was put in storage and not issued. British and Commonwealth forces were eventually supplied with 2,127 launchers and 86,000 bazooka rockets during the war, but they do not appear to have been commonly used in Europe. Details of the first shipment to the Red Army are obscure: Soviet histories do not mention any use at all even though 3,000 launchers and 8,500 rockets were sent during the war. Col Jarrett later claimed that it was one of the Whips sent to the Soviet Union in 1942 that was subsequently captured and served as the basis for the German *Panzerschreck* antitank rocket launcher. German accounts suggest it was American examples captured in Tunisia.

The haste to put the bazooka into service was largely due to US Army leaders wanting the new weapon in service by the time of Operation *Torch*, the invasion of French North Africa, in November 1942. Due to a combination of secrecy and a lack of time, most US Army units did not receive their Whips until aboard assault transports while at Hampton Roads, Virginia in October 1942. There had been no training or explanation about the weapons. The War Department training circular on the bazooka was not

published until December 15, 1942, and it was not widely distributed until after the Tunisian campaign. Some units, such as the 3rd Infantry Division, practiced with the weapons while at sea. The first recorded combat use of the Whip took place during the *Torch* landings by the 3rd Infantry Division, when bazookas were used against French coastal-defense bunkers and gun positions around Fedala. At least one French Renault FT light tank was engaged and destroyed by a bazooka used by the 3rd Infantry Division during the fighting around Fedala. The general reaction to the new weapon among the infantry troops was very favorable, but officers were extremely critical of the decision to issue a novel weapon without the provision of adequate training.

The bazooka was first noticed by the Germans during the fighting at Medjez el Bab in Tunisia in December 1942. Distribution of the bazooka in Tunisia was very uneven beyond the assault teams involved in the initial *Torch* landings. For example, the armored infantry of the 1st Armored Division did not begin to receive bazookas until late December 1942. In spite of the need for an effective antitank weapon, the general lack of information about the bazooka was a liability – a fact that would become painfully obvious during the US Army's stinging defeat at Kasserine Pass. Col Thomas Drake, commander of the 168th Infantry Regiment (34th Infantry Division), recalled the arrival of the first shipment of six truckloads of bazookas at their Sidi bou Zid positions on the night of February 12, 1943: "Distribution of these guns and rockets were made Saturday [February 13], but due to a lack of time for instruction, they were useless. Every effort had been made to get just one bazooka for instructional purposes, but without success. They had been systematically forwarded to front line outfits where they were just as religiously thrown away." Drake planned to institute a bazooka training class the next day, but before this occurred the Germans launched Operation *Frühlingswind*, the Kasserine Pass

One outcome of the German capture of numerous bazookas from the 168th Infantry Regiment at Sidi bou Zid in February 1943 was the rapid development of their own equivalent, the 8.8cm *Panzerschreck*, which went into use in October 1943. This was a larger weapon than the bazooka, with better anti-armor penetration. A captured example of the *Panzerschreck* is seen here in a display in Washington, DC during February 1944. The Tiger I heavy tank behind the four men was captured in Tunisia and is fitted with the *Nebelkerzen Wurfgerät* smoke dispenser on the left side of the turret, but it lacks the S-Mine discharger.

offensive, on February 14. Drake's regiment was overwhelmed by two Panzer divisions and he was taken prisoner. There was apparently little use made of the bazookas during the fighting, and this cache was probably the source of bazookas later sent back to Germany. Curiously enough, when the reconstituted 168th Infantry Regiment took the offensive in Fondouk Pass in Tunisia in April 1943, they were again issued bazookas only a day before the action and again without any training. The bazooka could have had an important role against the Panzers in this critical battle, but the opportunity was lost due to poor planning.

A variety of stories began to circulate in Tunisia in the hopes of encouraging a more positive attitude toward the new weapon. An Army history of the bazooka recalled these tall tales:

> One story tells of a detachment of ten enemy tanks which surrendered after several rockets scored near misses at long range. The tank commander explained that he thought he was in range of 105mm guns and that it was foolish to continue fighting. Another story is told of a soldier who knocked the turret completely off an enemy tank at 75 yards.

A team of military observers sent by Army Ground Forces offered a more sober assessment. "No sufficient battle experience data is available in this area to form an opinion ... The weapons had been recently issued and the men were not trained in their use." MajGen John Lucas reported that "I found evidence that several tanks had been knocked out by the 'Rocket' ... Apparently everyone is pleased with these weapons but their range is so short that they can seldom be used ... Something is necessary for the rocket launcher as men's faces are sometimes burned when firing." An observer from the Armored Force was more skeptical, reporting that he "could not find anyone who could say definitely that a tank had been stopped by bazooka fire."

By the time of Operation *Husky*, the invasion of Sicily in July 1943, training on bazooka operation had been instituted for units committed to the campaign. This paid immediate dividends when bazookas helped to stop German and Italian tank attacks against the Gela beachhead in the first days after the landing. An assessment prepared for Gen Eisenhower after the campaign deemed the bazooka "effective" and cited the example of one unit commander who stated that his unit had knocked out four PzKpfw IV tanks with bazooka fire.

The bazooka finally began to live up to its potential by the time of Operation *Shingle*, the landings at Salerno on the Italian mainland on September 9, 1943. The landing sites were attacked almost immediately by tanks of 16. Panzer-Division; and the attacks grew in intensity as the day wore on. The 2/141st Infantry in the center

Old versions of the bazooka remained in service in Italy due to the priorities for the planned landings in Normandy. Pictured on April 2, 1944 in the Anzio beachhead, this bazooka crew from the 2/30th Infantry (3rd Infantry Division) are still using an early-production M1 launcher without the Ordnance field modifications.

BAZOOKA SIGHTS

The M1 rocket launcher used a range ladder (**1**) at the front of the tube with four steps for 100yd, 200yd, 300yd, and 400yd. The rocket gunner would use the rear sight to select one of these ranges. By aiming with the bottom (400yd) sight, the gunner would then be elevating the launch tube sufficiently to account for the ballistic drop of the rocket at this range. The General Electric T43 bar sight (**2**) on the early M9 and M9A1 rocket launchers used a simple pip at the front of the sight, and a small peep-hole for the rear sight. Range adjustment was accomplished by rotating the bar sight against a simple scale on the side of the bazooka, with gradations from 100yd to 300yd. The Polaroid T90 reflecting sight (**3**) used the same range-adjustment method as the T43 bar sight and so was interchangeable with it. However, this used a 1× optical sight with etched reticle for aiming which was simpler to use. The T90 sight entered production in the autumn of 1944, and was used on subsequent production launchers. It could also be retrofitted to earlier M9 and M9A1 bazookas since it used the same screw attachment.

PANZER VISION BLOCKS

German tanks had a cupola for the commander fitted with a series of 1× periscopic sights for observing outside. The cupola on the PzKpfw IV Ausf J had five such sights. Each periscope was covered by an armored shutter, and the commander had to use a small handle within the cupola to open each of these. In reality, such sights did not offer a very good view of the surrounding terrain, particularly in the case of infantry under cover. This view shows a US bazooka team at a range of about 50m (55yd). Due to the limitations of these vision devices, Panzer tactics stressed the need for commanders to view the terrain from outside the cupola by leaving the hatch open and peering over the side. This of course put the Panzer commander at some hazard to infantry small-arms fire, particularly during street fighting when enemy infantry could snipe from the upper floors and attics of nearby buildings.

was hit by a tank attack in the morning, but the PzKpfw III and PzKpfw IV tanks were fought off using bazookas. Around 1020hrs, 13 tanks approached the 142nd Infantry Regiment command post, but the Germans were stopped by point-blank 105mm howitzer fire, losing five tanks in the process. The next attack came around 1145hrs and ran into a well-coordinated antitank defense consisting of bazooka teams of the 142rd and 143rd Infantry regiments, a T30 75mm self-propelled howitzer, two 105mm howitzers, and a 37mm antitank gun. This German attack was repulsed and eight tanks were knocked out. The 142nd Infantry Regiment later reported that the bazooka had proven to be "a really great defensive weapon," accounting for at least seven tanks during the day's fighting. The 1st and 3rd Ranger battalions knocked out two German armored cars with bazooka fire on the approaches to Monte di Chiunzi.

THE EUROPEAN THEATER

The bazooka was widely used in the European Theater of Operations (ETO) from D-Day through the final campaign in Germany. Since the US Army was on the offensive for most of this period, the bazooka was used as often as not as an offensive weapon, and it proved very popular with the infantry as a means to attack German strongpoints. Although originally developed as an antidote to the massed Panzer attacks of the Blitzkrieg era earlier in the war, there were very few such attacks in the ETO in 1944–45, and the Panzer attacks that did occur were usually on a much smaller scale.

In June 1944, most German Panzer units in Normandy were in the Caen sector facing British and Canadian forces. As the Wehrmacht responded to US Army advances, the first significant Panzer attack against US troops in Normandy was undertaken by the Panzer-Lehr-Division along the Vire River on July 11, 1944. This attack was repulsed mainly by M10 3in GMC tank destroyers. The American infantry soon realized that the bazooka was ineffective against the frontal armor of the new Panther tank and only marginally effective against the 80mm front hull armor of the PzKpfw IV Ausf H and Ausf J – but it was still effective against the thin side and rear armor of these tanks.

Nevertheless, the bazooka was still viewed as more useful in the *bocage* (hedgerow) country of Lower Normandy than the infantry's towed 57mm antitank guns, since engagement ranges were usually quite short due to the hedgerows, and because the 57mm guns were more difficult to move and maneuver in this type of terrain. Most infantry units attempted to accumulate more bazookas than authorized under the tables of organization & equipment (TO&E). When the new M9A1 bazooka arrived in 1944 to replace the older M1A1, many units kept the old bazookas since they were still perfectly functional in spite of their technical flaws. So for example, an infantry battalion had a nominal allotment of 29 bazookas under the TO&E, but the 1/9th Infantry at the time of the Krinkelt–Rocherath battle in December 1944 (described below) had at least 37 on strength.

The next massed Panzer attack against US forces in France was Operation *Lüttich*, the counteroffensive near Mortain starting on the night of August 6/7, 1944. This involved about 120 tanks and 32 assault guns and tank destroyers. Although bazookas played a role in the fighting, towed 3in antitank guns and artillery were more instrumental in halting the German attack. The 30th Infantry Division claimed to have knocked out 69 German tanks, but fewer than a dozen of these kills were credited

The bazooka played a secondary role in the fighting against the German Panzer counteroffensive at Mortain, Operation *Lüttich*, which started on the night of August 6/7, 1944. These two Panther Ausf A tanks and an SdKfz 251 half-track of 1. SS-Panzer-Division *Leibstandarte Adolf Hitler* were knocked out during the fighting against the 117th Infantry Regiment (30th Infantry Division) near Saint-Barthélemy.

to bazooka teams. The "Vosges" Panzer counterattack against Patton's Third US Army in Lorraine in mid-September 1944 was fought mainly against US and French armored divisions; bazookas played a minimal role in the defeat of this attack. As a result of the heavy Panzer losses in the summer of 1944, large-scale German Panzer attacks were very uncommon in the autumn 1944 fighting until the Ardennes offensive in December 1944.

THE OPPOSING SIDES

The Ardennes campaign in December 1944–January 1945 offers one of the few examples of an operational-level German offensive involving large numbers of tanks and armored vehicles against US infantry. The action investigated in this study is the three-day battle involving elements of the 2nd Infantry Division defending the 'Twin Villages' of Krinkelt–Rocherath against the attack of 12. SS-Panzer-Division *Hitlerjugend*.

THE AMERICAN DEFENDERS
During the fight for Krinkelt–Rocherath, the Lausdell crossroads would be defended by LtCol William Dawes McKinley's 1/9th Infantry plus other subordinate units. The defense of the villages themselves would be undertaken by Col Francis Boos' 38th Infantry Regiment, plus supporting armor from the 741st Tank Battalion and 644th

Tank Destroyer Battalion and towed antitank guns of the 801st Tank Destroyer Battalion. McKinley's battalion had suffered heavy casualties in the fighting around Wehlerscheid during December 13–16 and had gone from a strength of 713 men on December 13 to 409 men on December 16. Among the casualties, the battalion had lost four company commanders in its three rifle companies, and numerous platoon leaders and platoon sergeants. Fortunately, McKinley had conducted a special bazooka training program for his battalion prior to the December 13 mission, primarily because of the value of the bazooka in attacking the Westwall pillboxes in the Wehlerscheid area. In total, he had formed 22 bazooka teams. He had also stockpiled a further 15 bazookas with the battalion's Company D (heavy weapons). McKinley's attention to bazookas was due to his disdain for the 57mm antitank gun issued to infantry antitank companies. He felt that this weapon, a US copy of the British 6-pdr antitank gun, was ineffective in facing German tanks and far too cumbersome for foot soldiers to maneuver in close combat. Even though the bazooka was largely ineffective to penetrate a German tank frontally, he recognized that in the hands of a brave infantryman, the weapon could be maneuvered for a side or rear shot.

THE GERMAN ATTACKERS

The US defenders of the Lausdell crossroads and the Twin Villages would face battle groups formed from units of 12. SS-Panzer-Division *Hitlerjugend*, combining infantry from SS-Panzergrenadier-Regiment 25 with Panzer IV/70(V) tank destroyers of SS-PzJgAbt 12, PzKpfw IV and Panther tanks from SS-Panzer-Regiment 12, and other

A dramatic shot, probably taken in the Netherlands, of a Panther tank being hit by a bazooka rocket fired by a team of paratroopers on October 9, 1944. This was a staged event involving a wrecked Panther from Panzer-Brigade 107 knocked out in September during Operation *Market-Garden*.

PFC WILLIAM A. SODERMAN

William A. Soderman was born on March 20, 1912 in West Haven, Connecticut, and joined the US Army in August 1943. At the time of the battle for Krinkelt–Rocherath on December 18, 1944, he was a Private First Class in K/9th Infantry (2nd Infantry Division). During the initial fighting on the evening of December 17, his loader was wounded by artillery shrapnel. When a German armored column approached his position, Soderman stood up with his bazooka and hit the lead vehicle, disabling it and leading to its abandonment by its crew. Soderman's later Medal of Honor citation identifies these vehicles as "Mark V" (Panther) tanks, but they were more likely Panzer IV/70(V) tank destroyers of SS-PzJgAbt 12.

On the morning of December 18, Soderman was in a forward trench. Around dawn, the first wave of German tanks began moving toward the American lines. Soderman ran forward along a ditch toward the woods. He stood up at the last minute, firing a rocket at the lead tank and knocking it out. A deep ditch and the burning tank now blocked the exit from the woods and prevented the following four tanks from advancing any farther. On the way back to the K/9th Infantry positions, Soderman encountered a *Panzergrenadier* platoon moving through the fog, and fired at it with his rifle, hitting several and breaking up their advance. By 1000hrs, the German attack overran the A/9th Infantry positions in front of K/9th Infantry. The Medal of Honor citation describes Soderman's final action that day:

> By this time, enemy pressure had made Company K's position untenable. Orders were issued for withdrawal to an assembly area, where Pfc.

Pfc William A. Soderman receives the Medal of Honor from President Harry S. Truman at the White House on October 12, 1945.

Soderman was located when he once more heard enemy tanks approaching. Knowing that elements of the company had not completed their disengaging maneuver and were consequently extremely vulnerable to an armored attack, he hurried from his comparatively safe position to meet the tanks. Once more he disabled the lead tank with a single rocket, his last; but before he could reach cover, machinegun bullets from the tank ripped into his right shoulder. Unarmed and seriously wounded he dragged himself along a ditch to the American lines and was evacuated. Through his unfaltering courage against overwhelming odds, Pfc. Soderman contributed in great measure to the defense of Rocherath, exhibiting to a superlative degree the intrepidity and heroism with which American soldiers met and smashed the savage power of the last great German offensive.

Two US Navy ships have been named after Soderman. The first, a Danish commercial container ship of Maersk Line, was purchased by the US Navy and subsequently converted into to a large, medium-speed, roll-on/roll-off ship. T-AKR 299 was delivered to the Military Sealift Command in 1997 and christened as the USNS *Soderman*. In May 2000, USNS *Soderman* was transferred to the Maritime Prepositioning Force and renamed. As a result, when the eighth and final Watson-class roll-on/roll-off ship (T-AKR 317) was delivered to the US Navy in 2002, it became the second ship named after Soderman.

OBERLEUTNANT OTTO CARIUS

Otto Carius was a successful Tiger tank commander on the Eastern Front, and best known for his excellent autobiography, *Tigers in the Mud*. He was selected for this biographical sketch, not for his personal experience against the bazooka, but for his insightful comments on the issue of Panzer defense against close infantry attack.

Born on May 27, 1922, Carius initially served as a loader on a PzKpfw 38(t) light tank during Operation *Barbarossa* in the summer of 1941. In early 1943, he was sent back to Germany to train with the new Tiger heavy tank. During his service in northern Russia as a platoon leader in 1943–44, he and his crew were credited with destroying more than 100 Soviet tanks and similar numbers of Soviet antitank guns and field guns. Carius went on to lead a company equipped with the Jagdtiger tank destroyer. His unit saw very little combat against the US Army and surrendered in April 1945.

From his extensive combat experience in the Soviet Union, Carius developed a clear appreciation of enemy close-attack weapons. During fighting around Nevel in northern Russia in December 1943, he recalled an incident that illustrated both the shortcomings and occasional value of Soviet antitank rifles. After knocking out several Soviet antitank guns, his section began moving closer to Soviet defensive positions. The Soviet antitank riflemen began firing on his Tiger, trying to damage the view-slits. He recalled that "None of the vision blocks were functioning anymore after a short period of time." He instructed his section to halt, since the supporting infantry was nowhere to be seen. (A fundamental rule of German tank tactics was that tanks, and especially the expensive Tigers, were not to become mixed up in enemy infantry positions without the

Oberleutnant Otto Carius.

support of accompanying infantry.) Although his tank was equipped with the S-Mine discharger, he never put it to use: "A good Tiger Commander never resorts to using the close quarters weapon." His point was that the Tiger's principal defense against close attack was prudent tactics, not technological gimmicks.

Carius was awarded the Ritterkreuz des Eisernen Kreuzes mit Eichenlaub (Knight's Cross of the Iron Cross with Oak Leaves) by Reichsführer-SS Heinrich Himmler in October 1944. Himmler had heard many stories of the success of German infantry *Panzerknacker* troops, and he asked Carius whether tanks would soon be obsolete and ineffective due to the advent of new handheld antitank weapons. Carius replied:

I do not share this opinion … The Russians have used tank hunting troops for a long time. They have almost never achieved anything whenever our tanks were employed together and they supported each other. If infantry was present, it was even more difficult for them to accomplish anything. The probability of a hit with bazookas and similar weapons at greater distances is very small. If the tank crews are alert, then soldiers with those weapons can definitely shoot only one time. Panzerknacker teams have had an easy time with the British and the Russians whenever they operated with closed hatches.

Curiously, his one experience with an antitank rocket launcher was an "own goal" when, in April 1945, one of his Jagdtiger tank destroyers was hit by a *Panzerfaust* fired by a Volkssturm militia soldier in the Ruhr area.

Armed with an M9 2.36in bazooka, Pvt Robert Starkey of the 16th Infantry Regiment (1st Infantry Division) poses in front of a destroyed Jagdpanzer IV of 1./PzJgAbt 3 near Hamich that had been knocked out during Operation *Queen*, November 16/17, 1944. Starkey was credited with one of the three *Jagdpanzer* AFVs knocked out by bazookas that day, two more being credited to Pfc Carmen Turchiarelli.

divisional personnel such as combat engineers. Although Waffen-SS units had been elite formations in the summer of 1944, by the winter of 1944–45 they had deteriorated badly. Most of the experienced combat troops of the *Hitlerjugend* had been killed in Normandy, and the unit had been reconstructed in the autumn of 1944 with a mixture of conscripts and volunteers who were not especially well trained. By the evening of December 17, I./SS-PzGrRgt 25 had been badly beaten up in the fighting in the Krinkelterwald during the previous two days and had taken up defensive positions along the edge of the woods facing Krinkelt–Rocherath. December 17 also saw II./SS-PzGrRgt 25 suffer significant losses during the fighting in the woods. Owing to the inexperience of its troops, most officers were compelled to lead by example, and as a result, most had been killed or wounded during the day's fighting. Every company commander had become a casualty and many companies were now being led by NCOs. The regiment's third battalion, III./SS-PzGrRgt 25, was still on the march at this time.

THE STRATEGIC SITUATION

I. SS-Panzerkorps' attack in the Krinkelt–Rocherath sector was the *Schwerpunkt* (focal point) of the German Ardennes offensive. Two Waffen-SS Panzer divisions – 12. SS-Panzer-Division *Hitlerjugend* on the right flank and 1. SS-Panzer-Division *Leibstandarte Adolf Hitler* on the left – were assigned to break through this sector and race across the Meuse River near Liége. They were assigned to specific routes, designated as Rollbahn A through Rollbahn E. Krinkelt–Rocherath was the key crossroads on the northernmost route, Rollbahn A.

German tactics were standard for this period of the war, conducting the immediate penetration of enemy infantry defenses by infantry divisions, and waiting to inject the Panzer divisions for the exploitation phase once the breakthrough had been accomplished. This tactical doctrine recognized that Panzer divisions could easily become entangled in a costly attritional struggle with enemy infantry and lose their momentum, particularly due to the proliferation of infantry antitank weapons such as the bazooka. Following this doctrine, the attack in 12. SS-Panzer-Division's sector would begin with an attack by 277. Volksgrenadier-Division against the defensive positions of the 99th Infantry Division.[1] The plans anticipated that the *Volksgrenadiere* would reach and take Krinkelt–Rocherath on the first day of the attack, opening up the roads toward the Elsenborn Ridge for the Panzer advance.

In the event, the initial German infantry attack on December 16 did not progress as anticipated. Poorly trained, understrength, and poorly equipped, 277. Volksgrenadier-

---

1 This initial attack is covered in more detail in Steven J. Zaloga, *German Infantry vs US Infantry: European Theater of Operations 1944* (Osprey, 2015).

The 2nd Infantry Division's initial contact with German tanks took place around 0815hrs on December 17 when a small scout patrol from Kampfgruppe *Peiper* was engaged at Wirtzfeld by M10 3in GMC tank destroyers of the 1st Platoon, Company C, 644th Tank Destroyer Battalion, which knocked out two of the three PzKpfw IV Ausf J tanks. The German tanks were fitted with *Thoma-Schürzen*. Around December 17, three PzKpfw IV and some halftracks appeared about 600yd south of the 2nd Infantry Division headquarters outside Wirtzfeld. This wreck is being inspected by troops of the 9th Infantry Regiment's Antitank Company.

OPPOSITE The fighting for Krinkelt–Rocherath and the Lausdell crossroads, December 17–18, 1944.

Division was largely stymied for the first day in its attempts to penetrate the forested Krinkelterwald. SS-Brigadeführer Hugo Kraas, the commander of 12. SS-Panzer-Division, knew that a rapid race to the Meuse River was essential to the offensive and decided to inject elements of his own division into the fray earlier than recommended by standard tactical doctrine.

A *Kampfgruppe* from I./SS-PzGrRgt 25 under SS-Hauptsturmführer Alfons Ott began to push through the woods from Hollerath starting at noon on December 16. Although some penetrations of the woods were made by isolated groups, the roads were not yet clear for a mechanized advance. On December 17, the entire SS-Panzergrenadier-Regiment 25 was subordinated to 277. Volksgrenadier-Division to reinforce the attack. After a costly day of fighting, the battle groups of 12. SS-Panzer-Division began emerging from the Krinkelterwald after dark on the evening of December 17, more than a day behind schedule.

On the American side, the 99th Infantry Division managed to hold on to its defense line in the forest through the first two days of attack. At first, the V Corps headquarters that was responsible for this sector thought that the attacks on December 16 were simply a spoiling attack. North of this battlefield, V Corps had launched its own attack on December 13 around Wehlerscheid in yet another attempt to secure the Roer dams. Even as late as the morning of December 17, V Corps instructed its units to continue their offensive. However, the commander of the 2nd Infantry Division, MajGen Walter M. Robertson, was very agitated by the reports he was receiving from the neighboring 99th Infantry Division. He was very concerned that should the Germans capture the road junction at Krinkelt–Rocherath, both his own division and the 99th Infantry Division would be surrounded. Therefore, on his own initiative, he began moving reserve elements of his command back toward Krinkelt–Rocherath. The 3/38th Infantry was instructed to move to Krinkelt, while elements of the 23rd Infantry Regiment took up positions behind the 99th Infantry Division. Finally, the entire 9th Infantry Regiment was ordered to begin marching toward Wirtzfeld, to the west of Krinkelt–Rocherath.

During the course of December 17, MajGen Robertson continued to receive alarming reports on the intense fighting experienced by the 99th Infantry Division in the Krinkelterwald. He traveled to Krinkelt–Rocherath, and intercepted the 9th Infantry Regiment on its march to the southwest. The regiment was moving in a column with the 2/9th Infantry in the lead and the 1/9th Infantry at the rear. In the middle of the column, he instructed the HQ Company, 3/9th Infantry along with K Company to break off from the column immediately and set up a hasty defense of the Lausdell crossroads 2,000yd northeast of Rocherath. He then ordered LtCol McKinley's 1/9th Infantry to establish a defense of the Lausdell crossroads and to "hold the position at all costs" until ordered to withdraw. McKinley was authorized to take command of any units or stragglers withdrawing through the crossroads. The mission of the 1/9th Infantry was to shield the redeployment of the 2nd Infantry Division temporarily, so that it could establish a firm defensive base in Krinkelt–Rocherath and Wirtzfeld behind the badly damaged 99th Infantry Division.

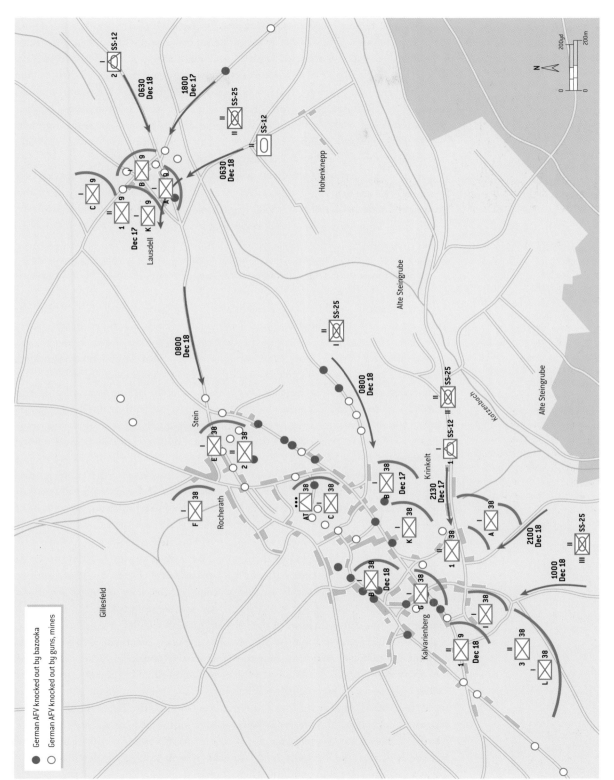

German AFV knocked out by bazooka

German AFV knocked out by guns, mines

McKinley, the grandnephew of US President William McKinley (served 1897–1901) and son of MajGen James F. McKinley, adjutant general of the US Army in the mid-1930s, had followed in his father's footsteps and graduated from the US Army Military Academy at West Point in 1937. McKinley's force consisted of his own battalion, the 1/9th Infantry, plus K/9th Infantry, 30 men of the 3/9th Infantry's HQ Company, and four M10 3in GMC tank destroyers of 2nd Platoon, Company A, 644th Tank Destroyer Battalion. In total, McKinley had about 515 troops at the Lausdell crossroads late in the evening of December 17. Capt Charles MacDonald, at the time a company commander in the 393rd Infantry Regiment and later a prominent US Army historian, encountered the 1/9th Infantry defenses that evening as his own unit retreated out of the Krinkelterwald:

> We came upon a group of dirty infantrymen digging in along a hedgerow. What people are these? There was supposed to be nothing between the Germans and Paris but our thin line of riflemen in the woods. I did not know who they were or what had brought them here, but they looked to me like dirty, bedraggled gods who had suddenly descended from the heavens to set this ridiculous situation straight. (MacDonald 1947)

McKinley knew he would be facing enemy tanks. Besides his specially trained bazooka teams, he depended on mines, and each of the main roads had antitank mines laid on either side. The roads themselves were left clear to permit the withdrawal of elements of the 99th Infantry Division from the neighboring woods. Once German troops appeared, special mine teams were instructed to pull "necklaces" of mines across the road.

The German formation exiting the woods shortly after dark on December 17 was from SS-Panzergrenadier-Regiment 25, commanded by SS-Sturmbannführer Siegfried Müller. To reinvigorate the attack on the evening of December 17, Müller created a new *Kampfgruppe* based around SS-Obersturmbannführer Richard Schulze's II./SS-PzGrRgt 25, supported by two Panzer IV/70(V) companies of SS-PzJgAbt 12 plus a *Pionier* (combat engineer) company. When the *Kampfgruppe* reached the edge of the woods, several Panzer IV/70(V) of 2./SS-PzJgAbt 12 were in the lead carrying small teams of *Panzergrenadiere* on their engine decks, followed by the remaining infantry troops of II./SS-PzGrRgt 25 on foot.

The weather that day was wet, with daytime rain and drizzle turning to snow after dark. The fields around the Lausdell crossroads were covered with 1–2ft of snow, but the ground was muddy and had not yet frozen solid. Tanks or other vehicles maneuvering off the roads ran the risk of becoming bogged down in the muddy fields, particularly if following other vehicles that had already churned up the soil. With temperatures hovering around freezing, a thick ground fog blanketed the fields. The executive officer of 1/9th Infantry, Maj William Hancock, described the visibility that evening as "practically nil" with snow showers mixed with fog.

Fortunately for the American defenders of the Lausdell crossroads, an artillery liaison officer attached to the regiment had been able to register targets on most of the roads with the supporting field-artillery battalions. Besides the division's own artillery battalions, the 1/9th Infantry was allotted the support of several corps artillery battalions during the course of the next 18 hours of fighting. The preregistration of the roads during the daylight hours substantially increased the lethality of the subsequent artillery strikes and proved vital to the defense of the crossroads.

COMBAT

NIGHT ASSAULT ON THE LAUSDELL CROSSROADS

Conditions around the Lausdell crossroads were chaotic. McKinley's force had barely had time to dig foxholes, and there was a disheartening stream of demoralized troops of the 99th Infantry Division filtering back toward Krinkelt–Rocherath. After dark, around 1930hrs, B/9th Infantry reported that three tanks and some infantry had passed through their lines. Although the company's acting commander, Lt John Melesnick, thought they were American, McKinley ordered A/9th Infantry to send a patrol. The tanks and infantry were in fact the spearhead of the advancing *Kampfgruppe*.

McKinley requested an artillery strike against the opening in the woods where the tanks and infantry had first appeared. Lt Stephen Truppner, commanding A/9th Infantry, reported that the barrage set one "tank" on fire and that the German troops "were screaming and had dispersed in all directions." A necklace of antitank mines was pulled across the road when the German vehicles were still about 400yd from the American lines. Two Panzer IV/70(V) struck the mines and were disabled when their tracks were blown off. Two more Panzer IV/70(V) drove off the road around the disabled vehicles, but both were knocked out by roving bazooka teams from B/9th Infantry. The combination of the ground fog and darkness made it possible for the American bazooka teams to approach the German vehicles very closely, especially if German infantry was not present.

An aerial view taken in April 1947, with Krinkelt to the left and Rocherath to the right. The Lausdell crossroads was located to the right, outside this image. The German attacks emanated from the woods outside this image to the bottom and the right.

SS-PzJgAbt 12 regrouped and launched another attack around 1840hrs. An artillery forward observer with A/9th Infantry directed fire against this column, reporting that four of the seven armored vehicles had been knocked out along with an undetermined number of infantry. B/9th Infantry reported the approach of yet another column emerging from the woods that appeared to be almost 1,000yd in length. The forward observer called in artillery on the head of the column, "walking" the fire back and forth for 10 minutes while .50-caliber heavy machine guns raked the columns. B/9th Infantry reported that "the night was filled with the screams of the wounded SS men." The German casualties included the company commander of 2./SS-PzJgAbt 12 and one of his platoon commanders.

In spite of the losses inflicted by US artillery, the *Kampfgruppe* continued to push toward Rocherath in the dark, often infiltrating the infantry-company command posts in the dark. The B/9th Infantry commander, Lt Melesnick, hunted down one of the Panzer IV/70(V)s with a bazooka around 2215hrs. One of the German tank destroyers that had been disabled with a broken track continued to fire at US positions with its main gun and a machine gun. Two GIs snuck up behind it with a 5-gallon jerry can of gasoline, placed it on the engine deck, and set it on fire with a thermite grenade. The resulting conflagration finally knocked out the stricken tank destroyer.

Another spasm of fighting broke out around 2230hrs when Kampfgruppe *Müller* attempted to coordinate the attack down all three forest roads. The artillery forward observer had difficulty calling in artillery fire on his radio due to German interference, but he finally got through and shouted "If you don't get it out right now, it will be too goddamn late!" He never received a reply due to further German radio interference, but three minutes later, the heaviest barrage of the night erupted all over the German lines. MajGen Robertson considered the defense of the Lausdell crossroads so essential that he assigned all four divisional artillery battalions plus three corps 155mm howitzer battalions to provide support.

When the fighting died down around midnight, McKinley had a field-telephone line laid from the Lausdell crossroads to the northeastern outskirts of Rocherath, defended by Col Francis Boos' 38th Infantry Regiment. Boos informed McKinley that the 1/9th Infantry would be subordinated to his command and that he expected that his battalion would be ordered to withdraw from the crossroads at some point the next day. By this time, fighting had erupted in Krinkelt–Rocherath.

Although the M9A1 bazooka was in widespread use by the time of the Ardennes campaign, many US units retained older M1A1 bazookas to increase the number available in rifle companies. The M1A1 continued to suffer from ignition problems due to battery shortages, however. This M1A1 in the hands of SSgt Robert Trevelin of the 1/329th Infantry (83rd Infantry Division) near Rochefort on January 6, 1945 has a pair of larger D-cell batteries jerry-rigged on the wooden shoulder-brace to circumvent the ignition problem.

THE INITIAL FIGHTING FOR KRINKELT–ROCHERATH

The defense of the "Twin Villages" of Krinkelt–Rocherath was assigned to 38th Infantry Regiment. LtCol Olinto M. Barsanti's 3/38th Infantry arrived in the vicinity on the morning of December 17 and set up its defense perimeter on the south side of Krinkelt to counter any German advance from Büllingen or Mürringen. LtCol Frank Mildren's 1/38th Infantry arrived next at the eastern end of Rocherath on the evening of December 17 and deployed to the north of the 3/38th Infantry in the fields on the eastern outskirts of Krinkelt–Rocherath. C/38th Infantry was badly hit by German artillery as it reached the outskirts of Rocherath and the survivors were incorporated into the defenses in the town set up by the regimental Antitank Company. The 1/38th

A pair of Panther tanks of 1./SS-PzRgt 12, knocked out in the positions of A/9th Infantry during the fighting in the early-morning hours of December 18. The tank to the left is Nr. 127 while the one of the right with the damaged track is Nr. 135, the mount of 3. Zug's platoon leader. (Darren Neely)

Infantry had not fully dug in when the first German attack commenced after dark. The last of the regiment's battalions to arrive was LtCol Jack Norris's 2/38th Infantry late on the night of December 17/18, starting with E/38th Infantry. This company was directed to assist the defenses centered upon the Antitank Company, while G/38th Infantry was assigned to the area around the regimental command post. Besides the rifle companies, the defenses included some divisional attachments with several M4 medium tanks of Company A and Company B, 741st Tank Battalion, towed 3in antitank guns of the 801st Tank Destroyer Battalion, and M10 3in GMC tank destroyers of the 644th Tank Destroyer Battalion. As at the Lausdell crossroads, the situation on the eastern outskirts of Krinkelt–Rocherath was chaotic, with a steady flow of demoralized troops of the 99th Infantry Division retreating into the town.

The first German attack against Krinkelt–Rocherath was preceded by an artillery bombardment. The *Kampfgruppe* assigned to attack the town consisted of SS-Obersturmführer Helmut Zeiner's 1./PzJgAbt 12 equipped with about a dozen Panzer IV/70(V) tank destroyers along with several companies of SS-Panzergrenadier-Regiment 25. The attack was staged from the woods east of the Twin Villages and hit the outskirts of Krinkelt–Rocherath shortly after dark. A/38th Infantry had been warned to expect an American M10 tank destroyer to retreat through their position, so when Zeiner's vehicles approached in the dark and fog, they were at first assumed to be American. However, when their identity became evident, they were brought under small-arms fire. The 1/38th Infantry lacked bazookas – the weapons were mostly in the battalion train which had not yet reached the town – and so the three Panzer IV/70(V) under Zeiner's immediate control passed over the A/38th Infantry foxholes, heading into the town. The accompanying *Panzergrenadiere* were engaged with small-arms fire, losing about 15 men. Unprotected by trenches, the neighboring B/38th Infantry was overrun by the German attack: the company commander, his command group, two rifle platoons, and one machine-gun section were captured or killed. The German attack reached as far as the village church, across the street from Mildren's 1/38th Infantry command post.

Zeiner's tank destroyers surprised three M4 tanks from Company A, 741st Tank Battalion and quickly knocked them out; then they shot up Mildren's command post and its associated vehicles. Surviving elements of B/38th Infantry retreated into the stone-built church. Close-range skirmishes with small arms continued in the dark streets. Capt Edward Rollings' C/38th Infantry was hit by a separate attack involving the two Panzer IV/70(V) and a platoon of infantry that had become separated from Zeiner's main group in the dark. Fighting engulfed this section of the town for about three hours. Due to the fog and dark, the conditions were extremely chaotic, with individual buildings changing hands repeatedly. The buildings were mainly of stone construction, making them ideal for defense.

The ferocity of the fighting subsided in the early-morning hours of December 18. Owing to the confusion, Zeiner withdrew 1./PzJgAbt 12 and the accompanying 40 *Panzergrenadiere* to the fields about 300yd outside the town in hopes of rejoining the rest of his unit and obtaining fuel and ammunition. Isolated groups of German infantry remained in parts of Krinkelt–Rocherath.

THE DAWN ATTACK ON THE LAUSDELL CROSSROADS

Berlin was furious about the delays in the vital *Hitlerjugend* sector, and insisted that the American defenses be crushed promptly. As a result, 12. SS-Panzer-Division decided to commit its tank battalion to the attack at dawn on December 18. SS-Sturmbannführer Arnold Jürgensen's I./SS-PzRgt 12 consisted of four tank companies: 1. and 3./SS-PzRgt 12 were equipped with Panther tanks and 5. and 6./SS-PzRgt 12 were equipped with PzKpfw IV Ausf J tanks. The Panther companies, carrying *Panzergrenadiere* on their engine decks, formed the spearhead of the attack. They were followed by the PzKpfw IV companies and surviving elements of II./SS-PzGrRgt 25 on foot. The only fresh infantry reinforcements were the men of III./SS-PzGrRgt 25, who were instructed to stage an attack on the left flank directly toward Krinkelt once they had arrived. Finally, Grenadier-Regiment 990 (277. Volksgrenadier-Division) was supposed to stage an attack on the right flank against elements of the 393rd Infantry Regiment (99th Infantry Division), still holding positions north of the Lausdell crossroads.

The temperature before dawn on December 18 was slightly above freezing, with a thick ground mist and drizzling rain. As a result, visibility remained poor. The Panther tanks of 1. and 3./SS-PzRgt 12 began moving forward from a clearing near Hill 627. In the early-morning light, the American bazooka teams were more vulnerable to fire from accompanying *Panzergrenadiere* than they had been the night before, and many bazooka teams were shot down before they could fire their rockets. The Panthers headed directly for Rocherath, overrunning A/9th Infantry. The *Panzergrenadiere* following the tanks then tried to clear the trenches and foxholes of surviving American infantry. Around 0900hrs, the A/9th Infantry commander, Lt Stephen Truppner, called McKinley and told him that his men had been completely overrun. Truppner requested that artillery "be poured on his own position because the situation was

PREVIOUS PAGES Soderman's
private war: Lausdell crossroads,
December 18, 1944.

hopeless anyway." He said his men "would duck in their foxholes and sweat it out." A US field-artillery battalion duly laid down a 30-minute fire mission on the A/9th Infantry positions, disrupting the German attack. Neither Truppner nor any of the men in the rifle squads escaped; fewer than a dozen men from A/9th Infantry's machine-gun squad survived the dawn battle.

The advancing tanks charged into the neighboring K/9th Infantry positions, and soon reached the only buildings at the Lausdell crossroads: the Palm family farm. A bazooka-man from K/9th Infantry, Pfc William Soderman, attacked one of the German tanks from close range, and knocked it out with a hit on the side. K/9th Infantry was swamped, and Capt Garvey surrendered his headquarters in the Palm farmhouse when a German tank advanced to within a few feet of the front door and began to take aim.

With A/9th Infantry and K/9th Infantry largely gone, the flow of German tanks continued between the remnants of McKinley's defense at the Lausdell crossroads and the northeastern outskirts of Rocherath. Around 1000hrs, another *Panzergrenadier* attack was directed against B/9th Infantry at the crossroads, leading to an intense small-arms battle. While this was going on, Boos telephoned McKinley and told him that he could withdraw his forces in about three hours at 1300hrs. A major artillery strike was promised to help defend the crossroads. However, McKinley warned Boos that he could not pull back to Rocherath because there were so many German tanks and troops in between. Shortly after this phone conversation, an officer of the battalion's Antitank Platoon spotted four M4 tanks of the 741st Tank Battalion operating on the northern side of Rocherath. Contact was made with the tank-platoon commander, Lt Gaetano Barcellona, who agreed to assist in the withdrawal. McKinley pointed out a group of four German tanks that were blocking the retreat.

As the artillery barrage began around 1115hrs, two of Barcellona's tanks maneuvered toward Rocherath, hoping to lure the four German tanks out of their blocking position. The other two Shermans remained near the crossroads in an overwatch position. The German tanks fell for the bait and maneuvered to intercept the two decoy Shermans. Barcellona knocked out two of the German tanks in quick succession, while the other two headed for the shelter of Rocherath. One was disabled by a hit to the rear and the last made it into the built-up area on the northern outskirts of Rocherath. With the path successfully cleared for withdrawal, McKinley's men began to retreat back into Rocherath; but when the battalion reassembled in the town later in the day, there were only 20 officers and 197 men present of the approximately 515 men who had defended the Lausdell crossroads. A/9th Infantry and K/9th Infantry had only one officer and 20 men from more than 200 at the start of the fight. McKinley's battalion had lost about three men out of every five in fewer than 18 hours of fighting. Nevertheless, the sacrifice of this battalion had given the 2nd Infantry Division time to erect a credible defense in Krinkelt–Rocherath. They had stymied the advance of SS-Panzergrenadier-Regiment 25, exposing the German infantry to prolonged artillery fire; and the heavy casualties suffered by the German infantry around the Lausdell crossroads would prove to be a critical ingredient in the failure of 12. SS-Panzer-Division's mission. McKinley later estimated that his battalion had accounted for 15–17 German tanks and tank destroyers, of which four were attributed to mines and the rest to bazookas. Capt Charles MacDonald of the 393rd Infantry Regiment, who had witnessed the defense, later wrote:

McKinley and the men of 1/9th and K Co., 3/9th had performed an incredible feat. By their stand, they had enabled two battalions of the 38th Infantry to reach the twin villages for a defense that otherwise probably could not have been mounted. "You've saved my regiment," Boos told McKinley. They had left the ground around the cluster of roads and trails and the [Palm] farmhouse littered with German dead and the carcasses of 17 tanks and tank destroyers. For all the pertinacity and valor displayed by a number of other battalions of the 2nd Infantry Division during the fight for the twin villages, none performed with more fortitude and sacrifice than the men of McKinley's battalion and K Co. And for all the defenses of many another American unit during the German counteroffensive, probably none exceeded and few equaled McKinley's battalion and K Co. in valor and sacrifice.

KRINKELT–ROCHERATH: PANZER GRAVEYARD

After having crushed the right flank of McKinley's defenses, I./SS-PzRgt 12 charged into Rocherath with the Panther tanks of SS-Obersturmführer Helmut Gaede's 1./SS-PzRgt 12 in the lead, followed closely by the Panthers of SS-Hauptsturmführer Kurt Brödel's 3./SS-PzRgt 12. This was a recipe for disaster. German doctrine recommended the use of *Panzergrenadiere* to support the tanks in a battle with enemy infantry, and tanks were certainly not expected to operate alone in a defended town against enemy infantry supported by hostile tanks. Two of the three battalions of

This Panther belonged to SS-Panzer-Regiment 12's reconnaissance platoon and was knocked out on the outskirts of Krinkelt–Rocherath during the fighting there on December 18. (Bill Auerbach)

SS-Panzergrenadier-Regiment 25 had already been decimated in the two previous days of fighting in the Krinkelterwald, however, and the artillery barrages around the Lausdell crossroads accounted for much of the remainder.

Around 0730hrs, the first wave of 11 Panther tanks raced down the main street of Rocherath. The regimental Antitank Company, led by Capt James Love, had its command post near the main street, and two bazooka teams intercepted the advancing German column and scored numerous hits against the tanks without stopping any. Moments later, the Panther column began to accordion as it reached the debris-clogged streets, and came to an abrupt halt. The Panthers had a small number of *Panzergrenadiere* riding on their engine decks, but the tank riders soon became casualties as the American infantry began peppering the tanks with small-arms fire and rifle grenades. Capt Love directed one of the M4 tanks of the 741st Tank Battalion down a side street so that it could engage one of the leading Panthers (Nr. 327) from the side; fire from the M4 quickly set the Panther on fire. The Panther behind it, Nr. 154, attempted to move past the burning tank, but Pvt Isabel Salazar from the Antitank Company positioned himself in a first-story window overlooking the street, and struck the second Panther with a bazooka rocket from a range of 200yd. The tank rolled forward alongside the first Panther before bursting in flames. The two burning Panthers blocked the street, forcing other tanks toward the rear of the column to extricate themselves from the traffic jam and move down side streets to reach Krinkelt. An hour later, Salazar scored another bazooka kill from his perch in the stone-built house when a Panzer IV/70(V) tank destroyer came to a halt behind the two knocked-out Panthers.

The surviving Panthers next encountered the defenses of 1/38th Infantry in the center of the Twin Villages and were peppered with small-arms fire. Several Panther tank commanders were wounded or killed by the small-arms fire, and the others buttoned up. The German tanks began shelling the US positions, especially the stone house near the church serving as a command post where several .30-caliber machine-gun teams were stationed. Unable to hit the American riflemen in the upper floors of the neighboring buildings, one Panther crew dismounted their coaxial machine gun, and fired it from the escape hatch in the rear of the turret. Two M4 tanks disabled the night before had been parked near their battalion's forward command post. Their guns were still functional, and they began to fire on the Panthers, eventually knocking out five. Two Panther tanks from 1./SS-PzRgt 12 moved past the burning wrecks; but when they reached the next intersection, they were engaged by one of the Antitank Company's five bazooka teams. A bazooka rocket struck the track of the lead Panther, halting its advance. The Panther was otherwise still intact, however, and continued to fire on the US riflemen. Even with the damaged track, the Panther could still pivot steer to give the hull machine gun a broader range of fire. One of the GIs found an M4 tank on a side street and directed it to a position near the beleaguered command post. The M4 fired a single round from about 200yd into the left side of the Panther's turret, destroying the tank. The fourth Panther was knocked out after being hit several times by bazooka rockets.

The fifth Panther of the group, Nr. 123, attempted to skirt around the wrecks but was hit repeatedly by bazooka fire, though none of the rockets penetrated. Two soldiers from the command post tried to prevent it from returning back into Rocherath and

opened up the gates of a cattle pen, stampeding a group of cows toward the tank. The Panther machine-gunned some of the cows, but decided against moving in that direction. Instead, it retreated back toward the company command post, crushing several jeeps on the way. A .50-caliber machine-gun team farther up the street kept it under a steady stream of fire, hoping to blind it by shattering its periscopes. The Panther crew was very concerned about the threat posed by the bazooka teams and finally managed to evacuate the area by driving down several alleys toward Krinkelt. The German tank eventually returned to the main road, and moments later encountered a jeep from the neighboring 3/38th Infantry which it ran over. A 57mm antitank gun from the 3/38th Infantry's Antitank Platoon hit the Panther in the turret, which began to rotate erratically, suggesting that the traverse motor had been damaged or the crew injured. The turret eventually froze to one side, and the Panther driver sideswiped two telephone poles with the gun barrel. The Panther raced past an M4 tank, which fired a single round but missed the fleeing tank. Several bazooka teams from M/38th Infantry tried to engage the Panther, but it was moving too quickly. The Panther finally managed to flee southward out of Krinkelt on the road toward Büllingen. An M10 3in GMC tank destroyer from 2nd Platoon, Company C, 644th Tank Destroyer Battalion near the 3/38th Infantry command post saw it, however, and fired three rounds through the thin rear armor, setting it on fire. A .50-caliber machine gun mounted on a jeep took the tank under fire, killing one or more of the crewmen; two crewmen were later captured by a bazooka team from M/38th Infantry. When inspected later, Panther Nr. 123 had 11 partial bazooka penetrations and several scars from 57mm impacts.

Willi Fischer, a Panther commander from 2. Zug, 3./SS-PzRgt 12, recalled the scene inside Rocherath:

> On 18 December 1944, we carried out the ill-fated attack on Krinkelt–Rocherath, a perfect "Panzer graveyard." The tanks of 1. Kompanie led the way, followed by our

A pair of knocked-out Panthers, Nr. 327 and Nr. 154, on the main street in Rocherath with the village water-tower evident behind. One of these tanks was knocked out when Capt James Love of the regimental Antitank Company directed an M4 Sherman tank against it from one of the side streets. The other was knocked out by a bazooka rocket fired by Pvt Isabel Salazar from a window of a house overlooking the street. (Darren Neely)

Kompanie under Brödel. I was lined up behind [SS-Oberscharführer Johann] Beutelhauser's tank, my Zug leader. When I got to the vicinity of the church, I saw a theater of horror. Beutelhauser's tank was hit in front of me. I could barely make out the position of the enemy antitank gun that hit him. Beutelhauser was able to jump off his tank and get to safety. I moved my tank to the protection of a house, unaware of what I would do next. Next to me was Brödel's burning tank; he was slumped lifeless in the turret. Along the road in front of me, all of the tanks had been knocked out and four of them were burning. Only one tank was still moving, I think Freier's, and it withdrew towards the battalion command post under my covering fire.

The surviving Panzer crews used this opportunity to withdraw under the protection of our tank, barely avoiding being taken prisoner by the encircling American riflemen. [Battalion commander] Jürgensen's tank showed up behind me. I was determined to get out of this hopeless situation and withdrew back beyond the cross-roads. But the cross-roads were targeted by the American antitank gun. The first round missed and the second struck the track and hull on the side. Luckily none of the crew was killed. The radio was wrecked and the track broken. I followed Jürgensen's instructions and backed up; the track slipped off and the tank bogged down once the road-wheels reached the mud.

While the fight between the antitank teams and the first Panther column took place on the eastern side of Rocherath, additional Panther and PzKpfw IV tanks from the other columns became engaged in a wild melee on the streets of Krinkelt and Rocherath with M4 tanks, M10 tank destroyers, and various infantry squads. By afternoon, the main German attack was exhausted due to heavy casualties; but there was still considerable fighting within the villages as well as attempts by small German battle groups to skirt the villages and head toward Büllingen and Wirtzfeld to the west. Besides the main attack past the Lausdell crossroads, another *Kampfgruppe* including the late-arriving III./SS-PzGrRgt 25 struck the 3/38th Infantry from the south at 1000hrs and again at 2200hrs. These attacks were halted with heavy artillery fire.

The *Hitlerjugend* losses on December 18, 1944 were so severe that I. SS-Panzerkorps was forced to change plans the following day. The need to open the roads to the Meuse had reached a critical stage. Although the German plans had expected the *Hitlerjugend* to reach the Meuse on the second day, they had in fact reached a depth of barely 10km (6 miles). On the evening of December 18, 1944, the focus of the *Hitlerjugend* attack was switched from Rollbahn A through Krinkelt–Rocherath to Rollbahn B through Butgenbach farther south, while the capture of Krinkelt–Rocherath would be left to 3. Panzergrenadier-Division and various follow-on infantry formations. However, the mission to open Rollbahn B would prove to be as frustrating as the battles against the 2nd Infantry Division. In the meantime, the US V Corps had reinforced the Butgenbach area with the 1st Infantry Division, and the fighting at the Dom Butgenbach manor during December 19–22 finally halted the 12. SS-Panzer-Division advance.

The 2nd Infantry Division held on to Krinkelt–Rocherath through the evening of December 19. The withdrawal to the Elsenborn Ridge began after dark. Possession of the Elsenborn Ridge rendered Rollbahn A virtually useless since it could be interdicted by the numerous field-artillery battalions entrenched in the heights above. Krinkelt–Rocherath was then occupied by elements of the battered 277. Volksgrenadier-Division; it was retaken by the 2nd Infantry Division in early February 1945.

STATISTICS AND ANALYSIS

How effective was the bazooka in anti-armor actions during World War II? The US Army never conducted any systematic study of this issue after World War II. Patton's Third US Army examined 130 knocked-out German tanks and found that the bazooka had been the cause of 17 (13 percent) of the losses. A broader assessment after the war concluded that German tank losses to shaped-charge weapons such as the American bazooka and British PIAT were about 4.5 percent of German tank casualties compared to about 11 percent of Allied tank casualties to German antitank rocket launchers. This difference was attributed to the defensive orientation of the German campaign as well as the larger number of German rocket weapons, especially the *Panzerfaust*, deployed in 1944–45.

From a purely technical standpoint, the bazooka was becoming obsolete by 1944 due to the increasing thickness of German tank armor. Yet the bazooka remained a popular weapon in infantry divisions. In reality, the US infantry had to cope with very few massed German tank attacks in 1944–45, and so the bazooka was seldom used in its intended role. Rather, its popularity stemmed from its versatility: it could be used to attack a wide range of targets including strongpoints, bunkers, and vehicles. Most infantry units preferred it to the towed 57mm antitank gun since its performance was not much worse in the antitank role, yet it was more compact and much easier to use in a wider range of combat scenarios. In total, US troops fired nearly 1.3 million bazooka rockets in the ETO in 1944–45, only a small fraction of which were directed against German AFVs. The bazooka probably knocked out only a few hundred German AFVs in the ETO, with the vast majority of bazooka rockets being used against targets of opportunity.

2.36in rocket launcher deployment and rocket expenditure in the ETO, June 1944–May 1945

Date	Launchers	Rockets expended
June 6–20, 1944	34,576	26,412
June 21–July 20, 1944	34,592	52,825
July 21–August 20, 1944	37,721	39,300
August 21–September 20, 1944	37,048	59,624
September 21–October 20, 1944	39,220	153,510
October 21–November 20, 1944	51,188	93,955
November 21–December 20, 1944	68,703	110,344
December 21, 1944–January 20, 1945	71,614	235,623
January 21–February 20, 1945	80,824	192,508
February 21–March 20, 1945	88,214	198,844
March 21–April 20, 1945	88,587	114,796
April 21–May 8, 1945	93,540	33,082
Total		1,310,823

Bazooka use was very extensive during the fighting in the Twin Villages during December 18–19. Nevertheless, bazooka performance was quite erratic, with many instances of failed ignition or failed detonation of the rocket warhead. There were numerous accounts of hitting German tanks with rockets that either failed to detonate, or failed to penetrate even if they did detonate. A skirmish with a Panther tank on the morning of December 19 involving troops near the company command post of C/38th Infantry is illustrative of these difficulties:

> Capt. Rollins yelled at [platoon leader Lt George] Adams to get a bazooka and finish off the enemy tank that was harassing him. Adams grabbed a bazooka himself, climbed

The Panzer graveyard inside Rocherath. This is the scene opposite the village church and in front of the Kalpers house on the main street. Panther Nr. 318 from 1. Zug, 3./SS-PzRgt 12 has been burned out and its barrel ripped off. This tank is often misidentified as belonging to the company commander, SS-Hauptsturmführer Kurt Brödel, but his tank was numbered 305 and was knocked out farther down the road.

into what was left of the attic. Sgt. Rudolph Kraft, second in command of the squad that was manning the house, got the second bazooka and joined Adams in the attic. Wanting to get increased effectiveness from a volume of fire, the officer and sergeant decided to fire a volley at the tank. They loaded and aimed and at the count of three, attempting to fire. Kraft's weapon discharged, but Adams' misfired. The sergeant's round hit the bogie of the tank. Adams, discarding the useless weapon, took over as loader for Kraft. The second rocket entered the top of the turret and burst against the inside. Adams was bending over to load a third round which probably saved his life when a high velocity shell hit the wall of the house and was quickly followed by a second. Adams was slightly injured when the remains of the wall collapsed on him, and he and Kraft withdrew to the safety of the cellar.

After the Krinkelt–Rocherath fighting, an ordnance officer of the 2nd Infantry Division was sent around to interview officers about the performance of their antitank weapons in the fighting. The towed 57mm antitank guns received almost universal condemnation as being both cumbersome to maneuver and ineffective against contemporary German tanks. The feelings about the bazooka were more positive, even if its limitations were clearly recognized. Major Utley, an infantry regiment S-3 (Operations), commented that "Our antitank company and our regiment have lost confidence in the 57mm gun as an antitank weapon, but our people strongly favor the bazooka for antitank work. Our men report that the antitank rifle grenades are ineffective against heavy tanks. We found that the new bazooka shell with the rounded nose has better effect than the older one with the pointed nose. I believe each rifle company should have seven bazookas."

Captain Joseph, S-3 of one of the infantry battalions, remarked that "We issued two extra rocket launchers to each rifle company so that each rifle platoon had two and the mortar section one. We have definitely stopped tanks with bazookas on several occasions. Our men know that the bazooka will not penetrate the Panther or the Tiger head on, but it is effective on the sides and rear of the tank or the turret." Captain James Love, who commanded the Antitank Company of the 38th Infantry Regiment, recalled that "I saw two Panthers knocked out with flanking fire from bazookas. One was 200 yards away, one was 150 yards. A Mark IV was knocked out at a range of 100 yards. On another occasion, at night, we fired four rockets from an upstairs window onto the top of a Panther or Tiger tank. All four rounds exploded, but did not stop that tank." Lieutenant Roy Allen, commander of B/9th Infantry at the Lausdell crossroads, remarked that: "I think the bazooka is satisfactory as is. We know that we must fire at the sides or the rear of the big tanks. I believe that five bazookas per rifle company is enough."

As part of an initiative to compare US and German weapons after the Ardennes fighting, the 2nd Armored Division interviewed a number of commanders about their opinions on various weapons. Lieutenant Colonel Russell W. Jenna, commander of the 41st Armored Infantry Regiment, offered these comments comparing the bazooka against its German counterpart, the 8.8cm *Panzerschreck*, as well as the smaller *Panzerfaust*:

From the tactical viewpoint, the German bazooka is better than ours due to the fact that it is bigger and packs a heavier punch. It is 88mm and ours is 2.36 in (60mm). It also

carries a windshield which makes the face mask unnecessary. There have been instances where our bazooka struck an enemy tank and failed to stop it. The German Panzerfaust is a fine weapon. It is light to carry and has absolutely no flash back which will harm the face or hands. It will easily make a large hole in four inches (100mm) of sloping armor. The Panzerfaust is easy to operate and seems to be very adaptable to inexpensive large scale manufacture. Our antitank weapons are all fine quality but need to be much heavier and more destructive. From an Ordnance viewpoint, while the German model is larger and has a more intricate firing device, its effectiveness and efficiency does not surpass out similar weapon. Many improvements have been made on the American model but even before these improvements and modifications it was just as good as the German model. The German gun being larger is more cumbersome and difficult to handle as well as store in a vehicle. The new American gun is rugged in construction and very accurate. The sighting mechanism on the German model is flimsy in construction and often faulty.

An M9 bazooka team from the 325th Glider Infantry Regiment (82nd Airborne Division) cover a road in Belgium on December 20, 1944 during the division's efforts to halt the advance of 1. SS-Panzer-Division.

Jenna's opinion was not universally shared. LtCol Louis W. Correll had troops of his 17th Armored Engineer Battalion test the bazooka against the *Panzerschreck* and his unit concluded that "the German bazooka is far superior to ours" due to much more reliable penetration of typical armored targets.

The fighting at Krinkelt–Rocherath on December 17–19, 1944 was chosen as the centerpiece of this study because it was one of the few occasions in the 1944–45 ETO campaign when the US infantry was faced with a massed Panzer attack. The bazooka was not the only weapon available for antitank defense, and was part of a combined-arms effort that included tanks, towed and self-propelled tank destroyers, as well as mines and field artillery. The bazooka clearly played a significant role in the battle, but statistical data on German tanks losses in the Krinkelt–Rocherath fighting are not clear from surviving records. The 2nd Infantry Division G-2 estimated German AFV casualties at

Krinkelt–Rocherath as about 70–80 tanks. The 38th Infantry Regiment estimated German losses as 67 German tanks and 300–400 enemy dead; the 1/9th Infantry estimated German armored vehicle casualties at the Lausdell crossroads as 15–17. The S-3 (Operations) of the 38th Infantry Regiment prepared a map of the locations of the knocked-out German vehicles after the battle and tallied 78 in the vicinity of the Lausdell crossroads and Krinkelt–Rocherath. A 1952 study by the US Army Office of the Chief of Military History using US unit records found that a total of 139 German AFVs were claimed to have been destroyed or knocked out of action during the Krinkelt–Rocherath battle. The study also concluded that this total was exaggerated by double claims. Of these unit claims, 37 (27 percent) were attributed to bazookas, including 11 by the 1/9th Infantry at the Lausdell crossroads, 24 by the 38th Infantry Regiment, and two by the 644th Tank Destroyer Battalion in Krinkelt–Rocherath. The other major causative agents were M4 tanks (49: 35 percent) and M10 tank destroyers (35: 25 percent).

Few German records regarding *Hitlerjugend* losses have survived. At the start of the Ardennes offensive, SS-Panzer-Regiment 12 had 78 tanks (41 Panthers and 37 PzKpfw IV); two weeks later, it had 20 operational tanks (seven Panthers and 13 PzKpfw IV). Total losses in December 1944 were 18 Panthers and eight PzKpfw IV, while a further 16 Panthers and 16 PzKpfw IV were disabled but recovered. Of these, most of the Panther casualties were suffered on December 17–19, while about half of the PzKpfw IV losses were suffered in the later Dom Butgenbach battle. Of its original 22 Panzer IV/70 tank destroyers, SS-PzJgAbt 12 lost three plus seven disabled but recovered. German AFV casualties during the battle of the Twin Villages were probably about 50 tanks and tank destroyers, of which about half were total losses and the remainder knocked out but recovered.

The statistics suggest that bazookas accounted for about one quarter of the German armored vehicles knocked out in the battle for Krinkelt–Rocherath. This was not typical of fighting in the ETO, where bazookas accounted for less than 5 percent of German tank casualties. The reason for the unusually high kill rate at Krinkelt–Rocherath was largely attributable to the battlefield circumstances. The defense of the Lausdell crossroads on December 17 was conducted at night in fog and snow showers. This rendered the German armored vehicle crews almost blind and allowed American bazooka teams to approach their targets from the side and rear at very close ranges without being spotted. The fighting inside Krinkelt–Rocherath on December 18 occurred during daylight, but the congested battlefield allowed the US infantry to hunt down the German tanks from the shelter of stone buildings that proved resistant to the Panzer's main anti-infantry weapon: its machine guns. Once again, German tank crews had a hard time defending themselves against the elusive tank hunters due to the battlefield circumstances. It is worth noting that the fighting between the 1st Infantry Division and 12. SS-Panzer-Division at Dom Butgenbach a few days later, conducted under quite different circumstances, saw bazookas play a less important role in the successful repulse of the final *Hitlerjugend* attack.

Regardless of the precise number of tanks knocked out in the Ardennes battles, the bazooka had a profound effect on infantry tactics, it being one of a number of infantry weapons that served as an antidote to the type of tank panic seen in the Blitzkrieg campaigns of 1939–41. Even though the infantry realized that their close-attack antitank weapons had only a limited chance of success in defeating tanks, their mere presence removed the sense of hopelessness suffered by infantry in 1939–41 in the absence of such weapons.

AFTERMATH

TOWARD THE "SUPER BAZOOKA"

Development of a more powerful bazooka was delayed by a lack of input from the combat theaters. The Army Ground Forces headquarters used the criteria of "battle-need" (meaning that new weapon programs were not approved unless troops in the field expressed a need for an improved weapon) and "battle-worthiness" as the cornerstone of their approval for new weapons. This process was fundamentally flawed

Besides the lack of "battle-need," the Artillery Development Division had taken over development of rocket launchers larger than 2.36in in 1942 with their T16 3.25in launcher. This was followed in 1943–44 with the improved T24 3.25in rocket launcher, shown here during trials at Aberdeen Proving Ground in May 1944. These designs were heavier and more robust than the existing bazooka, and were largely ignored by the infantry. The T24 project was terminated in September 1944.

since it presumed that units would forecast future armor threats. Through early 1944, there had been no indication from the Mediterranean Theater of Operations that better armor penetration was required. A delegation of officers called the New Weapons Board was sent to Europe in early 1944 to find out the opinions of troops about existing weapons and to gather input for future requirements. Troops in Italy were critical of the unreliability of the bazooka, but the New Weapons Board members were aware that this theater was still using old M1 and M1A1 bazookas with the old rockets because the newer M9 launchers and M6A3 rockets were reserved for the forthcoming campaign in France.

Encounters with the German Panther tank in France in July 1944 led to calls from the ETO for a bazooka with more punch. As a consequence of this request, development of the new T74 3.5in rocket launcher began in October 1944. The launcher was a scaled-up version of the M9A1 with a bipod for greater stability, while the rocket used a new propellant configuration that offered higher speed and greater accuracy. The enlarged warhead shifted to a copper liner and so increased penetration to 11in (280mm) compared to the 4in (100mm) of the previous 2.36in rockets. Trials by the Infantry Board in April 1945 found the new launcher to be satisfactory, but the rocket needed more attention. An initial batch of 5,000 launchers was ordered in August 1945 to support an anticipated invasion of Japan, but the end of the war led to a termination of production beyond test batches. The new "super bazooka" was standardized in October 1945 as the M20 3.5in rocket launcher, but production was deferred for several years due to lack of funds. The M20 would see its combat debut in Korea in 1950 after the M9A1 2.36in bazooka proved inadequate against North Korean T-34-85 medium tanks.

TANK DEFENSE SINCE 1945

The German efforts at defending against close-attack weapons have many echoes in modern armored vehicle design. Smoke-grenade launchers, for example, have become ubiquitous. These were not peculiar to German tank design, and indeed it can be argued that British smoke-grenade launchers during the war were more sophisticated and a closer predecessor of modern designs. Remote-control weapon stations (RWS) have also flourished, these being a more sophisticated evolution of the *Rundumsfeuer*; and the *Nahverteidigungswaffe* has given way to active protection systems (APS), aimed at defeating RPGs and antitank missiles with special munitions. Curiously enough, they present some of the same problems as their World War II German predecessors, especially concern over potential fratricide of nearby friendly infantry. *Thoma-Schürzen* have given way to a variety of slat armor types. While slat armor might seem to be directly equivalent to *Schürzen*, today's slat armor defeats modern RPGs by a fundamentally different process that exploits issues with the piezoelectric fuzes of modern RPGs – a technology not found on the World War II bazooka or *Panzerfaust* rocket. Small-arms designers have remained intrigued by the Rheinmetall curved-barrel weapon, but this concept has not re-emerged beyond experimental designs.

OPPOSITE   The M9A1 2.36in bazooka proved inadequate in combat in the summer of 1950 and was replaced by the M20 3.5in "super bazooka." These two soldiers of the 26th Infantry Regiment compare the much larger M20 on the left with the smaller M9A1 on the right at Grafenwöhr, West Germany in August 1950.

FURTHER READING

This account of the development of the bazooka is based primarily on Ordnance development records as well as the numerous reports of the Infantry Board at Fort Benning, Georgia. These records are located at the National Archives and Records Administration II at College Park, Maryland. The map showing German tank casualties in Krinkelt–Rocherath is based on the map of the S-3, 38th Infantry Regiment, located in the Combat Interviews collection at NARA II. The accounts of the development of German defenses against close attack were compiled from numerous books on German tank development, especially the "Panzer Tracts" series by Tom Jentz and Hilary Doyle, along with a variety of Allied technical intelligence reports located at NARA II.

The battle for Krinkelt–Rocherath has been the subject of at least two US Army studies. In addition, there is extensive detail on the battle in the 2nd Infantry Division section of the Combat Interviews collection in Record Group 407 at NARA II. The After-Action Reports for the 2nd Infantry Division, as well as its supporting tank and tank-destroyer battalions, were also examined, and these are also in RG 407 at NARA II. Records of 12. SS-Panzer-Division for the Ardennes campaign have not survived in any abundance.

US GOVERNMENT REPORTS

Anonymous (1943). *Technical Manual TM 9-294, 2.36-Inch A.T. Rocket Launcher M1A1*. US Army, September 1943.

Anonymous (1944). *Rockets and Launchers All Types*. Ordnance School, Aberdeen Proving Ground: February 1944.

Anonymous (1945a). *The Rheinmetall Borsig Works & Proving Grounds Unterluss*. Combined Intelligence Objectives Sub-Committee.

Anonymous (1945b). *US Rocket Ordnance Development and Use in World War II*. Office of Scientific Research and Development.

Anonymous (1946). *Record of Army Ordnance R&D, Volume 2: Small Arms and Small Arms Ammunition, Book 3: Machine Guns and Special Weapons*. Office of the Chief of Ordnance.

Baily, Charles M. et al. (1991). *Anti-Armor Defense Study Final Report, Volume IV: US Antitank Defense at Krinkelt-Rocherath, Belgium (December 1944)*. US Army Concepts Analysis Agency.

Coox, Alvin & L. Van Loan Naisawald (1951). *Survey of Allied Tank Casualties in World War II*. Operations Research Office, Johns Hopkins University.

Gregg, Annie (1948). *Project Supporting Paper Relating to Rocket Launchers World War I thru World War II (1917–August 1945)*. Small Arms Division, US Army Ordnance Department.

Karamales, Lloyd J., et al. (1990). *Anti-Armor Defense Study Final Report, Volume II: US*

Antitank Defense at Mortain, France (August 1944). US Army Concepts Analysis Agency.

Thompson, Royce (1952a). *Dom Butgenbach Action, 26th Inf. (1st Div.), 19–22 December 1944*. Office of the Chief of Military History.

Thompson, Royce (1952b) *Tank Fight of Rocherath-Krinkelt (Belgium) 17–19 December 1944*. Office of the Chief of Military History.

Walters, William (2007). *Introduction to Shaped Charges*. US Army Research Lab.

Walters, William (2008). *A Brief History of Shaped Charges*. US Army Research Lab.

OTHER SOURCES

Anonymous (1980). "Schürzen: zur Verstärkung der Panzerung," in *Waffen Revue*, Nr. 40.

Berger, Hagen (2013). *Panzerknacker: Grenadiere im Nahkampf gegen Kolosse aus Stahl*. Taching: Verlag für Wehrwissenschaften.

Burchard, John (1948). *Rockets, Guns and Targets: OSRD Science in World War II*. Boston, MA: Little, Brown.

Carius, Otto (2003). *Tigers in the Mud*. Mechanicsburg, PA: Stackpole.

Cavanagh, William (1985). *Krinkelt-Rocherath: The Battle for the Twin Villages*. Boston, MA: Christopher Publishing.

Cavanagh, William (2004). *The Battle East of Elsenborn & the Twin Villages*. Barnsley: Pen & Sword.

Denny, Harold (1944). "US Battalion's Stand Saves Regiment, Division, and Army," in *New York Times*, December 31, 1944.

Fedoseyev, Semyon (2002). *Pekhota protiv tankov: protivotankovye sredstva blizhnego boya v 1939–1945 gg*. Moscow: Tekhnika i vooruzhenie.

Fedoseyev, Semyon (2014). *Istrebiteli tankov vtoroy mirovoy*. Moscow: Yauza.

Gander, Terry (1998). *The Bazooka: Hand-Held Hollow-Charge Antitank Weapons*. London: Parkgate.

Laemlein, Tom (2014). *Bazookas and Flamethrowers*. Rochester, NY: Armor Plate Press.

Macdonald, Charles (1947). *Company Commander*. Washington, DC: Infantry Journal Press.

Meyer, Hubert (1994). *The History of the 12.SS-Panzerdivision Hitlerjugend*. Winnipeg: Fedorowicz.

Sohns, Armin (1968). "Anti-tank rifles," in *AFV News*, Vol. 3, No. 3, May 1968: 9.

Vannoy, Allyn & Jay Karamales (1996). *Against the Panzers: United States Infantry versus German Tanks 1944–45*. Jefferson, NC: McFarland.

Weeks, John (1975). *Men Against Tanks: A History of Antitank Warfare*. New York, NY: Mason/Charter.

Wijers, Hans (2009). *Battle of the Bulge, Volume 1: The Losheim Gap/Holding the Line*. Mechanicsburg, PA: Stackpole.

Another Medal of Honor action involving the bazooka during the Battle of the Bulge took place on December 21, 1944. Pfc Francis S. Currey from the 120th Infantry Regiment (30th Infantry Division) began stalking tanks of Kampfgruppe Z, Panzer-Brigade 150 near Malmedy. This unit, part of Otto Skorzeny's ill-fated Operation *Greif* (Griffon) involved the use of Panther tanks disguised to look like American M10 tank destroyers. Currey was credited with three tanks that day and later awarded the Medal of Honor. This illustration shows him besides one of his victims, a burning *Ersatz* M10.

INDEX

Monet | Kelly

Essays by Yve-Alain Bois
and Sarah Lees

Clark Art Institute
Williamstown, Massachusetts

Distributed by
Yale University Press
New Haven and London

Monet | Kelly

Published on the occasion of the exhibition
Monet | Kelly, Clark Art Institute, Williamstown,
Massachusetts, November 23, 2014–
February 15, 2015

Produced by the Publications Department
of the Clark Art Institute, 225 South Street,
Williamstown, Massachusetts 01267
clarkart.edu

Thomas J. Loughman, *Associate Director*
Anne Roecklein, *Managing Editor*
Dana Pilson, *Interim Managing Editor*
Dan Cohen, *Special Projects Editor*
Walker Downey, *Publications Intern*

Copyedited by Sharon Herson
Designed by Studio Blue, Chicago
Proofread by Lucy Gardner Carson
Color management and printing by
Puritan Capital, Hollis, New Hampshire

Monet | Kelly is organized by the Clark Art
Institute. The exhibition is made possible by the
generous contribution of Denise Littlefield Sobel.
Additional support is provided by Agnes Gund,
Marie-Josée and Henry R. Kravis, and Emily Rauh
Pulitzer.

Distributed by Yale University Press,
302 Temple Street, P.O. Box 209040,
New Haven, Connecticut 06520-9040
yalebooks.com/art

Printed and bound in the United States
of America
10 9 8 7 6 5 4 3 2 1

Library of Congress Cataloging-in-Publication
Data

Monet | Kelly / Essays by Yve-Alain Bois and
Sarah Lees.
    pages cm
    "Published on the occasion of the exhibition
Monet | Kelly, Clark Art Institute, Williamstown,
Massachusetts, November 23, 2014–February 15,
2015."
    ISBN 978-1-935998-20-4 (sterling and francine
clark art institute, publisher : alk. paper)—
ISBN 978-0-300-20787-3 (yale university press,
distributor : alk. paper) 1. Kelly, Ellsworth, 1923–
—Exhibitions. 2. Monet, Claude, 1840–1926
—Exhibitions. 3. Monet, Claude, 1840–1926
—Influence—Exhibitions. I. Bois, Yve-Alain.
II. Lees, Sarah. III. Sterling and Francine Clark
Art Institute.

N6537.K38A4 2014
759.13—dc23

2014037185

Cover Illustrations
Front: Claude Monet, *The Path under the
Rose Arches* (detail of cat. 7); back: Ellsworth
Kelly, *Tableau Vert* (detail of cat. 14)

Details
Pages 10–11: Claude Monet, *Storm on the
Coast of Belle-Île* (cat. 2)
Pages 28–29: Henri Manuel, photograph of
Claude Monet in his Giverny studio, 1920
Pages 48–49: Ellsworth Kelly, *Tableau Vert*
(cat. 14)
Pages 60–61: Photograph of Ellsworth Kelly
on Belle-Île, 1949

While many know Ellsworth Kelly for his reimagining of abstraction through bold color and graphic innovation, few are familiar with his direct engagement with Claude Monet's work, first while he lived in postwar France, and then episodically over the decades that followed. During his formative years – a time during which Kelly's trajectory diverged from other American artists in the wake of World War II – he confronted and responded particularly to Monet's late works. Kelly's reaction to seeing Monet's water-lily paintings resulted in his first monochrome, *Tableau Vert*, which he painted the day after visiting Monet's studio in 1952. Yet he equally appreciated the older artist's compositions of windswept seascapes at Belle-Île, a place Kelly first visited in 1949. In both 1965 and 2005, Kelly returned to Belle-Île on artistic pilgrimages to work in the same locations that Monet had frequented previously. Kelly has similarly mined the work of Monet's fellow modernist pioneers Matisse and Cézanne on trips through France.

Monet | Kelly brings Kelly's work together with a number of particular Monet paintings that inspired him, demonstrating a rich intergenerational link. The concept of the exhibition emerged from conversations with Diego Candil and Vanessa Lecomte, our colleagues at the Musée des Impressionismes, Giverny, and with Joachim Pissarro. At the Clark the project has been overseen by Richard Rand, along with Sarah Lees and Nathan Stobaugh. In addition, Jack Shear, Eva Walters, and Mary Anne Lee provided crucial guidance and assistance all along the way.

Foreword

Above all, I thank Ellsworth Kelly for his extraordinary vision in conceiving the exhibition, choosing the works, and designing the installation. This has proven a marvelous opportunity for the Clark to work with a great living artist as both curator and exhibitor. I would also like to thank Yve-Alain Bois and Sarah Lees for contributing their insightful essays to this catalogue and our associate curator for contemporary projects, David Breslin, for his valuable insight and services as a key liaison. We are particularly grateful to Marianne Mathieu at the Musée Marmottan Monet in Paris, and to our colleagues at the Art Institute of Chicago, the Minneapolis Institute of Arts, and the Art Gallery of New South Wales in Sydney for lending the paintings by Monet, as well as to Ann Temkin and Phyllis Hattis for their crucial assistance at the last minute. Without their cooperation this project would not have been possible. My deepest gratitude extends to those benefactors who have supported this effort, foremost Denise Littlefield Sobel, whose leadership gift has made *Monet | Kelly* possible. We are also grateful to Agnes Gund, Marie-Josée and Henry R. Kravis, and Emily Rauh Pulitzer for their additional support. Finally, to all who contributed to this exhibition and catalogue, our appreciation is only matched by the gratification in having achieved, as the Clark so often does, a special level of thoughtfulness and experience for our visitors and readers alike.

Michael Conforti
Director

My first contact with Monet's late work was a painting of water lilies (*Nymphéas*) in May 1952 at the Kunsthalle in Zürich. Although I had been living in Paris since 1948, I had never visited the Musée de l'Orangerie where Monet's large mural of the *Nymphéas* (his gift to France after the end of World War I) was installed after his death in 1926.

Returning from Zürich to Paris, I found a book on Monet by his close friend Georges Clemenceau, the Premier of France, in which I learned that Monet had lived and worked in Giverny. My knowledge of Monet's work ended with the Haystacks, and I knew nothing of his work after 1900.

In August of 1952 I wrote Monet's stepson Jean-Pierre Hoschedé who invited me to make a visit to Giverny. A friend and I took a train to Vernon, then walked several miles along a dirt road where we found the property. Entering the main house, in the entry room there were early landscapes and a painting of the English Parliament. I said, "These are nineteenth century; what was done after 1900?" Hoschedé said, "Come, I'll show you." He took us out to the gardens and to the large glass studio, which Clemenceau had helped Monet build in 1917. I remember there were a couple of broken glass panes, some pigeons flying around, and a lot of leaves on the floor. At that time the French art world didn't appreciate Monet's late work.

Artist's Statement

And there they all were. There must have been fifteen enormous paintings, twenty feet long. I was very impressed. I had never seen paintings like this: overall compositions of thickly applied oil paint representing water with lilies, with no skyline. I felt that these works were beautiful, impersonal statements.

In 1951, I had begun to make paintings made up of joined panels, with each color on its own canvas, with only color and form as the content. I wanted to make visually engaging, impersonal works. Seeing the *Nymphéas* affirmed what I was doing.

The day following the trip to Giverny, I painted *Tableau Vert* (cat. 14), my first monochrome. I had already made works with many color panels, but to make one color on a canvas was a challenge.

Monet's last paintings had a great influence on me, and even though my work doesn't look like his, I feel I want the spirit to be the same.

Ellsworth Kelly
12/08/2001

Monet
Places and
Process

Sarah Lees

The work of Claude Monet (1840–1926) is frequently categorized by its subject matter, which covers a wide range of sites and objects, from the steam-filled shed of the Gare Saint-Lazare to grainstacks ablaze with setting sunlight to the lively surface of his lily pond in Giverny. From early in his career, however, Monet made comments suggesting that his art was not just an objective record of natural phenomena but also the result of his subjective response to the scene before him. "What I will do here [in Étretat]," he wrote to fellow artist Frédéric Bazille as early as 1868, "will be simply the expression of what I have felt personally.... The further I go, the more I see that one never dares express openly what one feels."[1] While the formal manifestation of this subjectivity is apparent in most of his painting, it became more pronounced in his later years. From at least the period of the series paintings onward, the material qualities of his canvases – the infinite subtle or dramatic variations of color and touch, the gradual diminishment of illusionistic space and increasing emphasis on physical surface – carry perhaps even greater weight than any overt content or ideological or philosophical implications they may contain. From this perspective, the process and material of representation take on greater significance, distinct from the subject represented.

It was just these material qualities that were reevaluated in the 1950s, leading to a revival of interest in Monet's late work as representing a type of lineage for contemporary, explicitly abstract, work.[2] The gestural, expressive brushstrokes and large-scale canvases of such artists as Jackson Pollock, Clyfford Still, Willem de Kooning, and Barnett Newman were easily compared with Monet's painting. This sort of parallel, however, would seem to exclude Ellsworth Kelly, whose work most often features uninflected surfaces of flat color or taut, unshaded lines in drawings and prints. In fact, Kelly and a number of somewhat younger artists also drew inspiration from the Impressionist master, if in a different manner, one less easily visible on the surface.[3]

This exhibition sheds additional light on the significance of Monet's work for Kelly by investigating a group of Kelly's drawings that have not previously been published – drawings that foreground geographical place as an element in the dialogue between Kelly and earlier artists. Kelly spent August and September of 1949 on Belle-Île, an island off the southern coast of Brittany where Monet had made his own four-month trip sixty-three years earlier. And in 1952, he made a pilgrimage to the French artist's abandoned studio in Giverny, where many of the post-1900 paintings that were later bequeathed by the artist's son to the Académie des Beaux-Arts were stacked indiscriminately against the walls.[4] On subsequent trips to France in 1965 and 2005, Kelly revisited Belle-Île and purposefully retraced the steps, and motifs, of the artist who preceded him.[5] In selecting works by Monet for this exhibition, then, Kelly sought out two distinct groups of paintings – those made on Belle-Île in 1886, and those depicting the gardens at Giverny, made during the first two decades of the twentieth century. While the sites thus coincide with

Kelly's own travels in France, there is no explicit link within Monet's output between these two groups of works. Nonetheless, considering them together can help to draw out not only the developments that occurred in Monet's painting between 1886 and the later period, but also some of his concerns that remained constant.

In early September of 1886, Monet and his companion (and later wife) Alice Hoschedé returned from the spa town of Forges-les-Eaux, a short distance north of Giverny, where Alice had gone for treatment of an illness. After announcing his wish to head for Étretat, where he had labored the previous fall and winter over a group of some fifty-one views of the resort town's famous arched cliffs and needle rocks, Monet had a sudden change of heart. On September 12, he wrote to his dealer Paul Durand-Ruel to announce his arrival on the island of Belle-Île.[6] For at least a year, Monet had been considering going to Brittany, although unlike Paul Gauguin, who had begun his first stay in the Breton town of Pont-Aven just a few months earlier, in July 1886, Monet was not motivated by a desire to find a simpler, more "primitive" culture and society.[7] Instead, he went in search of dramatically unfamiliar landscapes, even leaving the relative comfort of a hotel in the island's main town of Le Palais after a couple days, deeming the location uninteresting. "I'm going to install myself in a little hamlet of eight or ten houses, close to the place called the Terrible Sea, and it's aptly named: not a tree for ten kilometers around, rocks, admirable caves; it's sinister, diabolical, but superb, and since I don't think I'll find such a place anywhere else, I want to try to make a few canvases here," he wrote to Alice on September 14, in his second letter to her from the island.[8]

Belle-Île was not quite as isolated and unpopulated as Monet had anticipated. After just five days on the island he met another artist, Australian-born John Peter Russell, and about a month after that he first made the acquaintance of critic Gustave Geffroy, who would go on to become a great supporter and the author of the first biography of Monet. Despite such sometimes-welcome distractions, the thirty-eight paintings Monet made on Belle-Île, much like those he had painted at Étretat, never acknowledge the existence of modern life and the growing tourist industry. Rather, they focus exclusively on the dramatic cliffs, inlets, and needle rocks of its coastline, and the wide-ranging and sometimes extreme weather conditions under which he viewed them.[9]

While Le Palais was on the northeast, mainland-facing side of the island, where wide, sandy beaches could be found, the village in which Monet had taken up residence, Kervilahouen, was on the southwest, unsheltered side, a short distance inland from the steep cliffs and dramatic needle rocks on the shoreline at a location called Port-Coton.[10]

14

Fig. 1 Claude Monet, *Rocks at Belle-Île*, 1886. Oil on canvas, 59.5 × 73 cm. Ny Carlsberg Glyptotek, Copenhagen

These formations became the first motif to draw his attention. Six canvases center on one dark, twisted rock accompanied by a strikingly attenuated smaller companion, the space between them so narrow that they might almost have been sliced apart vertically at a single blow. In some of the canvases the distinctions between solid, fluid, and void very nearly blur, the dark rocks contrasting so sharply with the brilliant water that they almost look like negative empty space. The paintings are concerned as much with the colors of the ocean, however, as with the weather-beaten forms of the rocks. In *Rocks at Belle-Île* (fig. 1), the water consists of thick, almost unmixed touches of emerald green and cobalt blue, topped by a lattice of pure white foam. The rock formations are distinctly reminiscent of the Porte d'Aval and needle rock at Étretat (fig. 2), but such a parallel, consciously chosen or not, may have helped the artist begin to grapple with a subject he otherwise felt he had not experienced before. "It's superb," he commented to Alice, "but it's so different from the Channel that I need to familiarize myself with this nature; the sea is utterly beautiful, and as for the rocks, they're a pile of grottoes, headlands, and extraordinary needles, but as I told you, I need time to learn how to grasp that."[11] The other five canvases of this location, viewed from the same elevation at the edge of the cliff, are recombinations of the same elements: the intense blue-green water lightly accented with white on a calmer day, or nearly covered over with foam in more agitated weather; the granite needles taking on an ominous, blue-black or green-black tinge under a certain light, or a warm ocher-beige when directly illuminated.

Around a headland to the southeast of Port-Coton is Port-Goulphar, another site where Monet set up his easel to make a group of related canvases. Two of these, *Port-Goulphar, Belle-Île* (cat. 3) and *Rocks at Port-Goulphar, Belle-Île* (cat. 1), show the artist making slight adjustments to his viewpoint and framing of a composition. *Port-Goulphar, Belle-Île* is a vertical canvas painted in full sunlight, where again the predominant colors are emerald and cobalt, with darker touches of forest green in the shaded hollows of the rocks. Another color that elsewhere serves as an accent comes to the fore in the horizontal *Rocks at Port-Goulphar, Belle-Île*, a dark wine-red covering much of the central rocks, highlighted with a few points of brighter crimson. For the vertical canvas the artist seems to have situated himself partway down the cliff face on which he was working, so that the jagged edges of rock next to him encroached on his perspective from both sides while the top of the central massif on which he focused rises above the distant cliffs behind it. In the horizontal painting he is slightly more elevated, suspended above the foreground water and looking down on the forms in front of him, which fall just under the line of the distant cliffs. Despite these differences, the two works are complementary in their broad outlines,

17

Fig. 2 Claude Monet, *Cliffs at Étretat*, 1885.
Oil on canvas, 65.1 × 81.3 cm. Clark Art Institute,
Williamstown, Massachusetts

as the Y shape formed by the wedge of water in *Port-Goulphar, Belle-Île* finds an echo in the similarly shaped shadow cast by the central rock in *Rocks at Port-Goulphar, Belle-Île*, the dark and light values reversed from one work to the other.

For about eleven days in early October, the weather was so stormy that Monet could scarcely work at all. He could still walk along the cliffs, though, and on these outings it was precisely the colors of the ocean that he particularly noted. "I've never seen such a raging sea, yet even in its fury it still has its lovely green and blue color."[12] A few days later he wrote to Alice that "the tempest has redoubled in violence; it's extraordinary to see the ocean; what a spectacle!… It has begun to lose a little of its emerald color from being so agitated; how I wish you were here to see it!"[13] By the end of this period he had managed to get five views of the raging sea, including *Storm on the Coast of Belle-Île* (cat. 2). Each again features the jagged black rocks located at Port-Goulphar, here nearly buried under roiling, foam-covered waves. Monet's observations are evident in this painting, as the tones of blue-green persist but in modified form, shifted from emerald toward turquoise. Another work in the group, *Storm off the Coast of Belle-Île* (fig. 3), predominantly white and beige with a few streaks of olive, also indicates that the sea had indeed "begun to lose a little of its emerald color." The radically independent, violently energetic brushstrokes of *Storm on the Coast* reveal its genesis as a rapid sketch that the artist was able to dash off while battling the elements. It very effectively conveys the turmoil of the storm, showing the solid rocks covered with blue streaks of water, which cause them to lose their sharp outlines and look almost fluid under the onslaught, while dashes of white foam reach toward or even over the tops of the cliffs. Monet commented many times in his letters from Belle-Île that he started canvases outdoors before the motif, but would finish them later in his studio, sometimes during bad weather. Often his impatience at being stuck indoors was exacerbated by dissatisfaction with such reworked paintings; in one instance he reported having put in at least twenty separate sessions before deciding he had spoiled the canvas and scraping off all the paint.[14] But these images of stormy weather, while they were surely the products of more than one work session, successfully retain the immediacy and energy of the artist's initial experience.

Like the Belle-Île works, the paintings of the 1900s in this exhibition (cats. 4–9) are similarly focused on a single site: Monet's garden in Giverny. Monet first moved to Giverny in 1883, bought the house he had been renting in 1890, and purchased additional land in 1893 that included a pond he would transform into his famous water garden. With the exception of several painting campaigns in London between 1899 and 1904 and one in Venice in 1908, virtually all of his twentieth-century canvases

18

Fig. 3 Claude Monet, *Storm off the Coast of Belle-Île*, 1886. Oil on canvas, 65 × 81.5 cm. Musée d'Orsay, Paris

depict aspects of his garden. Working in a location with which he was intimately familiar, with a relatively limited range of motifs and weather conditions, Monet explored the potential of the series format and the nature and materials of the painting process to the fullest extent of his career in these works. He no longer felt the need to seek out unfamiliar terrain or extremes of nature, and his accumulated wealth and his growing international fame meant that he no longer depended on selling as much new work as possible. Instead, he focused intently, almost obsessively, on the components of his art – the shaping of his pond and plantings, the format and framing of his views, his choice of paint colors, the character and placement of each brushstroke. As Paul Hayes Tucker noted of a group of water-lily paintings made between 1903 and 1907, "divorced from commercial concerns and rigorously limited in subject matter, they can be considered, on one level at least, to be largely concerned with picture making, with how an artist constructs pictorial problems and goes about solving them."[15] Given the freedom his situation afforded him, Monet could also keep paintings with him rather than selling them, whether because he considered them unfinished or simply because he wished to be able to refer to them as he continued to work. Indeed, all of the six later works in this exhibition remained with the artist until his death, and then passed to his son Michel.

These six works can be divided into three distinct motifs. *Water Lilies, Study* (cat. 4) belongs to a series of fifteen water-lily paintings of 1907 that share a vertical format and a clearly fixed vantage point.[16] As its title suggests, it is probably an unfinished canvas, and certainly the sketchiest and least heavily worked of the group. Nonetheless, the underlying composition is evident, anchored by an S curve of light blue strokes that traverse the center-left of the canvas and shade into darker blue spreading across the bottom. This basic shape is repeated very closely in each of the fifteen paintings, which vary only slightly in their proportions. While the two-dimensional layout is relatively straightforward, the three-dimensional representation this series explores is far more complex. As the eye travels from the top to the bottom of the canvas, it traces a path simultaneously from a point close to the edge of the pond in the distance to the clump of lily pads in the nearby bottom foreground, and, in the space reflected on the pond's surface, from the trees at the water's edge into the sky high overhead. Every part of the image is both near and far at the same time; the curls of green paint in the lower quarter of the canvas represent the point closest to the viewer, while the strokes of darker blue immediately next to them stand for the area farthest away. The one element that varies widely in this series, and that is relatively lacking in *Water Lilies, Study*, is light. Monet probably would have worked up the pale, unsaturated colors of this sketch into a version of the wide-ranging hues of the related works, in some of

Fig. 4 Claude Monet, *Water Lilies (Nymphéas)*, 1907. Oil on canvas, 92.1 × 81.2 cm. The Museum of Fine Arts, Houston. Gift of Mrs. Harry C. Hanszen

which the blue sky is cool and silvery (fig. 4), while in others it is entirely replaced by the blazing yellows and oranges of the setting sun.

The dynamics of reflection that characterize *Water Lilies, Study* reappear in a later approach to the pond, but in drastically altered form. *The Water-Lily Pond* of 1918–19 (cat. 5) is a horizontal canvas that centers on the water's edge, where branches overhang the surface. The colors here are heightened to a non-mimetic point, however; the water and much of what may be background foliage are figured primarily in strokes of red and fuschia. Bursts of green more logically suggest a weeping willow, but its reflection appears as vertical strokes of orange, flecked with a few touches of green. The relation between the willow and its reflection, established only tenuously by the placement and directional nature of the brushwork, nonetheless provides the key to the composition, linking the more densely applied paint in the upper half of the canvas with the open facture in the lower half. Three-dimensional space opens around this linkage, as it defines the horizontal surface of the water and the location of the foliage above and at a slight distance from that surface, within a field of color that would otherwise appear to coincide with the flat vertical face of the canvas.

In the next group of later works – two *Japanese Bridge* paintings (cats. 6 and 9), and the closely related *Path under the Rose Arches* (cat. 7) – assertive color becomes the principal component, and the complex spatial dynamics of the lily-pond paintings are no longer present. Even two-dimensional shape and three-dimensional form are subsumed into the tangles of thick, intensely colored brushstrokes that cover these canvases. All three date to about 1918–24, a period when color was in fact of the utmost concern to Monet, as well as to observers of his paintings.[17] The artist had become aware of cataracts in both eyes affecting his vision in about 1912, and after resisting the idea for many years, he finally underwent three rounds of surgery to his right eye in 1923. The cataracts reduced Monet's visual acuity and affected his color perception, and may account to some extent for the intensity of color and remarkably broad handling in these works. His compositional abilities, however, remained unaffected. Each of these three works focuses tightly on an arching form that spans the canvas nearly from edge to edge. This form, surrounded by abundant growth, vaults over a lower layer made up of either earth and foliage or water and aquatic plants that looks as substantive and solid as the arch itself. Changing light effects are no longer explored, again perhaps due to Monet's compromised vision both before and after his surgery, and pictorial space is reduced to a minimum, with recession into depth hinted at only by the tunnel-like shape created under the arch. The more horizontal format of the Minneapolis work encompasses a few

22

Fig. 5 Henri Matisse (French, 1869–1954), *Belle-Île*, 1896. Oil on canvas, 50 × 73 cm. Private collection

more partially identifiable details, including a blue and green clump of plants at the lower left and a passage of long vertical strokes along the right side that may represent willow branches, but aside from these elements, the expressive power of these works is carried almost entirely by pure color and the dynamic energy of Monet's brush.

Weeping Willow (cat. 8), one of three similar canvases, dates to about the same period, when, as Monet commented, "the colors no longer had the same intensity for me … my painting was getting more and more darkened."[18] As in the bridge and rose-trellis paintings, pictorial space is minimized here, and the sprays of dark green, purple-blue, and light blue that pour down the center of the somber-hued canvas suggest the title subject primarily because such trees appear more recognizably in other works, rather than because the colors and brushstrokes represent a willow beside his pond in any legible way. This painting as much as any of Monet's late works comes close to abstraction, nearly, but not quite, disconnecting color and form from a referent in the world.

It is just these elements, of color, form, and physical object or place, that intertwine in different ways in the works by Kelly that reference Monet. The line drawings made on Belle-Île are concerned with place and with shape, as they outline exactly the same monolithic cliffs, rocks, and the voids between them, from the same vantage point, as Monet had earlier painted – and in two instances, rocks recorded by Henri Matisse, who was himself following in Monet's footsteps to the island (cats. 25 and 26; fig. 5). The deep blue and green of the ocean that had so enthralled Monet, however, is omitted. This omission is emphatically underscored in *White Curve in Relief over White (Belle-Île)* from 2013 (cat. 29), which Kelly connected with the site of his own first experience of Belle-Île; it uses pure, colorless form, unbounded even by a defining line. Curiously, coincidentally, Monet's Belle-Île colors emerge instead in a different work that resulted from Kelly's pilgrimage, made three years after his stay in Brittany, to the other location identified with Monet: his Giverny studio. "The day after I visited Giverny," Kelly commented, "I painted a green picture, a monochrome" (*Tableau Vert*; cat. 14).[19] But that painting consists not of a single color but of a field of intermingled blue and green touches. Here form is omitted, just as it very nearly was in the paintings of Japanese bridges, rose trellises, and water lilies that Kelly had seen the previous day at Giverny.

As most analyses of his works indicate, Kelly's primary method consists of basing his abstractions on "already-made" aspects of physical objects in the world, and unlinking their components of shape, color, and identity or geographical specificity.[20] Kelly described his own process as "deciding what I didn't want in a painting, and I just kept throwing things out – like marks, lines, and the painted edge."[21] Considering Monet's paintings in the context of the methods Kelly developed on the French artist's ground helps to highlight the ways in which the same elements intertwine, if perhaps more closely and uniformly, in Monet's

24

work. There is a distinct congruence between the two artists' search for inspiration. In seeking out the rocks of Belle-Île, Monet was searching not only for an unfamiliar locale, but also for forms that were, in a sense, more purely forms than celebrated landmarks, as the immediately identifiable cliffs of Étretat were.[22] In his handling and framing, the rock formations appear simpler, more monolithic, and the compositions less narrative, less filled with incident, than most of his other paintings. Color, too, is heightened and emphasized, and it came to predominate in his late work, in which color serves as the primary structuring element while form is essentially vestigial. Linda Nochlin has suggested that Kelly can be seen as "a major incarnation of the nineteenth-century [French] vanguard's unpredictable future." Her point of comparison was Edgar Degas, whom, she noted, "Kelly made me think of … differently."[23] While Degas and Monet are quite dissimilar, Monet's work presents another type of comparison, and it, too, can be thought of differently. For the Monet paintings that Kelly has chosen also point to a process of throwing things out; they suggest the possibility of unraveling their component elements even if they don't fully follow through by discarding them. But that follow-through is just the kind of unpredictable future that Kelly's work embodies.

Daniel Wildenstein's *Claude Monet: biographie et catalogue raisonné*, 5 vols. (Lausanne and Paris: La Bibliothèque des Arts, 1974–91) is the standard reference for works by Claude Monet. Throughout the current publication, paintings by Monet are cited according to Wildenstein's catalogue (abbreviated as "W") number.

1 Claude Monet to Frédéric Bazille, Dec. 1868, in Wildenstein, *Claude Monet* (1974–91), 1:425–26, letter 44: "Ce que je ferai ici ... sera simplement l'expression de ce que j'aurai ressenti, moi personnellement.... Plus je vais, plus je m'aperçois que jamais on n'ose exprimer franchement ce que l'on éprouve." Monet was commenting on his pleasure at being able to respond directly to nature in Étretat, rather than to the pressures of the Parisian art scene.

2 See Michael Leja, "The Monet Revival and New York School Abstraction," in *Monet in the Twentieth Century*, Paul Hayes Tucker et al., exh. cat. (Boston: Museum of Fine Arts; London: Royal Academy of Arts, 1998), 98–108.

3 As Ann Gibson first argued in "Things in the World: Color in the Work of U.S. Painters during and after the Monet Revival," in *Monet and Modernism*, ed. Karin Sagner-Düchting, exh. cat. (Munich: Prestel, 2001), 111–41.

4 Kelly described this visit, which was prompted by his curiosity about "what ... happened to Monet in his last years," in an interview with Paul Taylor, published in *Interview* 21, no. 6 (June 1991): 102.

5 In 2000, he also went to Aix-en-Provence, and made drawings of Mont Sainte-Victoire, one of Paul Cézanne's favored motifs.

6 Claude Monet to Paul Durand-Ruel, 12 Sept. 1886, in Wildenstein, *Claude Monet* (1974–91), 2:275, letter 684. Belle-Île was some 530 km southwest of Giverny, rather than the 140-km journey northwest to Étretat.

7 As Steven Z. Levine has suggested, Monet's motivation may have been in part quite literary; Gustave Flaubert's *Par les champs et par les grèves* included a paean to the sublime beauty of the island, which he had visited in 1847, and had just been posthumously published earlier in 1886. See Levine, "Seascapes of the Sublime: Vernet, Monet, and the Oceanic Feeling," *New Literary History* 16, no. 2 (Winter 1985): 377–400. Denise Delouche notes that Monet owned a copy of this book. See Delouche, *Monet à Belle-Île* (Douarnenez: Le Chasse-Marée/ArMen, 1992), 18.

8 Claude Monet to Alice Hoschedé, 14 Sept. 1886, in Wildenstein, *Claude Monet* (1974–91), 2:276, letter 686: "Je ... vais m'installer dans un petit hameau de huit ou dix maisons, près de l'endroit appelé *la Mer Terrible*, et c'est bien nommé: pas un arbre à dix kilomètres à la ronde, des rochers, des grottes admirables; c'est sinistre, diabolique, mais superbe, et, ne croyant pas retrouver pareille chose ailleurs, je veux essayer d'y faire quelques toiles."

9 These paintings are W 1084–1121. One other painting made on Belle-Île, W 1122, depicts Poly (François Hippolyte Guillaume), the former fisherman who carried Monet's equipment during much of his time on the island. See also Daniel Wildenstein, *Monet: Catalogue raisonné* (Cologne: Taschen, 1996), 1:226–27.

10 As Gustave Geffroy explained in an article, "Each of these indentations [in the shoreline] ... is given the name of *port* in the language of the island. Yet very few are actually used to harbor boats. Only Port-Goulphar, irregular and contorted, offers the necessary depth and safety." See Geffroy, *Pays d'Ouest* (Paris: Bibliothèque-Charpentier, 1897), 254; this translation from Wildenstein, *Monet* (1996), 3:414.

11 Claude Monet to Alice Hoschedé, 18 Sept. 1886, in Wildenstein, *Claude Monet* (1974–91), 2:276, letter 688: "C'est superbe, mais c'est si différent de la Manche qu'il me faut me familiariser avec cette nature; la mer est de toute beauté, quant aux rochers c'est un amas de grottes, de pointes, d'aiguilles extraordinaires, mais comme je vous le dis, il faut du temps pour savoir prendre cela."

12 Claude Monet to Alice Hoschedé, 11 Oct. 1886, in Wildenstein, *Claude Monet* (1974–91), 2:280, letter 708: "Jamais je n'avais vu la mer aussi démontée et tout en étant furieuse, elle conserve sa belle couleur verte et bleue."

13 Claude Monet to Alice Hoschedé, 15 Oct. 1886, in Wildenstein, *Claude Monet* (1974–91), 2:281, letter 713: "La tempête a redoublé de violence; c'est extraordinaire de voir la mer; quel spectacle!... Elle commence à perdre un peu de sa couleur d'émeraude; que je vous voudrais là pour voir cela!"

14 Claude Monet to Alice Hoschedé, 14 Nov. 1886, in Wildenstein, *Claude Monet* (1974–91), 2:289, letter 746.

15 Paul Hayes Tucker, "The Revolution in the Garden," in *Monet in the Twentieth Century*, 45.

16 These paintings are W 1703–17.

17 It is difficult to date these paintings precisely, although most sources agree on an approximate range. Wildenstein lists them so as to suggest that Monet worked on both motifs during overlapping periods, the bridges from 1918 to 1924, and the trellises from 1920 to 1922. See Wildenstein, *Monet* (1996), 4:912–29. Both groups seem to have been referenced, Wildenstein proposed, in Joseph Durand-Ruel's comment of October 1923 that "it is clear that [Monet] cannot see anything anymore and cannot even take account of color" (ibid., 4:912).

18 The comments date to 1918 and were published by François Thiébault-Sisson in "Claude Monet's Water Lilies," *La Revue de l'art ancien et moderne* (June 1927), reprinted in Charles F. Stuckey, ed., *Monet: A Retrospective* (New York: Hugh Lauter Levin, 1985), 290.

19 *Interview* 21, no. 6 (June 1991): 102.

20 In his frequently cited description of the development of this process, Kelly stated that "everywhere I looked, everything I saw became something to be made, and it had to be made exactly as it was, with nothing added…. The subject was there already made." Cited in Yve-Alain Bois, *Ellsworth Kelly: The Years in France, 1948–1954*, exh. cat. (Washington, D.C.: National Gallery of Art, 1992), 184. It is perhaps also coincidental that he made this discovery in 1949, in the same period he first visited Belle-Île. Indeed, some of his first object-paintings were inspired by things observed on Belle-Île, such as *Kilometer Marker*, 1949 (San Francisco Museum of Modern Art), and the initial sketch and then gouache of *Window I*, 1949 (both private collection).

21 *Interview* 21, no. 6 (June 1991): 102.

22 For a discussion of the importance of his choice of identifiable motifs at Étretat, see Robert Herbert, *Monet on the Normandy Coast: Tourism and Painting, 1867–1886* (New Haven and London: Yale University Press, 1994).

23 Linda Nochlin, "Kelly: Making Abstraction Anew," *Art in America* (March 1997): 71–72.

Monet
Paintings

1
Rocks at Port-Goulphar, Belle-Île
1886
Oil on canvas, 66 × 81.8 cm
The Art Institute of Chicago

2
Storm on the Coast of Belle-Île
1886
Oil on canvas, 59.7 × 72.4 cm
Private collection

3
Port-Goulphar, Belle-Île
1887
Oil on canvas, 81 × 65 cm
Art Gallery of New South Wales, Sydney

4
Water Lilies, Study
1907
Oil on canvas, 105 × 73 cm
Musée Marmottan Monet, Paris

5
The Water-Lily Pond
c. 1918–19
Oil on canvas, 73 × 105 cm
Musée Marmottan Monet, Paris

6
The Japanese Bridge
c. 1918–24
Oil on canvas, 89 × 100 cm
Musée Marmottan Monet, Paris

7
The Path under the Rose Arches
c. 1920–22
Oil on canvas, 92 × 89 cm
Musée Marmottan Monet, Paris

8
Weeping Willow
c. 1921–22
Oil on canvas, 116 × 89 cm
Musée Marmottan Monet, Paris

9
The Japanese Bridge
c. 1923–25
Oil on canvas, 88.9 × 116.2 cm
Minneapolis Institute of Arts

Retracing
Monet

Yve-Alain Bois

Claude Monet and Ellsworth Kelly form an unlikely pair. Whenever Kelly responded to Monet, as this exhibition makes clear, he produced works that were exceptions in his oeuvre. This raises at least two questions. First: What happens when an artist comes into contact with the work of another whose aesthetic is almost antipodal to his? And second: What happens when he tries to put himself in the other's shoes?

Perhaps nothing reveals the chasm separating Monet's and Kelly's respective aesthetics more clearly than this declaration by the American artist reflecting upon his discovery of ten or so large *Nymphéas* canvases during his visit to Monet's Giverny studio, which he dates to August 1952: "I had never seen paintings like this: overall compositions of thickly applied oil paint representing water lilies, with no skyline. I felt that these works were beautiful, impersonal statements."[1] "Impersonal statements!" How easily can one imagine Monet wincing at such a counter-intuitive appreciation of his work!

And yet, it is precisely Kelly's tireless quest for impersonality during the three years preceding his encounter with Monet's late paintings that made him so receptive to them. To be sure, they were a far cry from what Kelly was doing at the time. The impasto, the heavy and swirling brush-strokes, and the fact that, albeit tenuously, these are still figurative works: all that makes them foreign to his pictorial universe. To be sure, once again, artists often prefer more what looks very different from their own production to what resembles it most. (It was Mondrian, after all, who convinced Peggy Guggenheim to take Pollock seriously – examples of this sort abound.) But what Kelly noted about these paintings is telling: they are "overall compositions" and there is "no skyline" in them.[2] The first formulation is a bit of an oxymoron since one of the essential properties of the all-over strategy is to provide an escape from the con-ventions of composition, from what Frank Stella called the "relational aesthetic" that characterized the tradition of postwar European abstract art and that Kelly was finding so tedious at the time when touring the Parisian art galleries.[3] But the oxymoron is apt: those late *Nymphéas* paintings are *not yet* quite all-over; they still comprise some composi-tional aspects, they still perform a balancing act – though ever more tenuous. The second observation, "no skyline," is even more pertinent: what Kelly noticed is the absence of one of the most important elements of landscape painting, the horizon, which anchors our human percep-tion. No skyline means there is nothing much to guide you in space, no real possibility to assert distance or scale. In some of these Monet late works, even the floating water-lily flowers and leaves that provided some spatial cues are on the verge of disappearance.

Such paintings are almost like walls – or rather clouds – of vibrating colors, without any point of focus: those are the works that would be suddenly rediscovered a few years later by the art world, particularly in New York in the wake of Abstract Expressionism. Kelly had come to them a bit earlier, and through a different route (which is not surprising, given that

while living in Paris, he barely knew what was happening on the other side of the Atlantic). The route was different, and so were the effects of the encounter. As Michael Leja has established, in the mid-fifties the Abstract Expressionist painters – and their admirers – recognized in the late canvases of Monet the works of an ancestor who retrospectively conferred legitimacy on them.[4] (In other words, they did not learn from Monet; they welcomed him, after the fact, as a grand supportive ally.) There was no such feeling of recognition on Kelly's part (his own work was too different from what he saw in Giverny), but, on the contrary, a sense of bewilderment whose force led him to swerve for a very brief moment from his trajectory. What is particularly striking is that his immediate pictorial response – *Tableau Vert* (cat. 14) – looks more like the works of New York painters of the Abstract Expressionist generation (I am thinking of the quivering surface of certain Newmans or Rothkos of the period) than anything he had ever painted or would ever paint. "The day following the trip to Giverny, I painted *Tableau Vert*, my first monochrome," writes Kelly.[5] Calling it a monochrome is slightly mis-leading (it all depends on how good you are at optical mixing, for the painting definitely includes shades of both blue and green bleeding into one another). Though textureless, it has nothing to do with the plain fields of solid, unadulterated vivid color that had been part and parcel of Kelly's pictorial language since 1950: it has modulations, it softly vibrates on its own. Yet it features no image, no drawing, no division, no shape other than that of the whole pictorial field itself – and in that sense it is much more a monochrome than any painting by Newman or Rothko.

53

Tableau Vert was undoubtedly an emotional response to the kind of oceanic awe that Kelly experienced at Giverny. For a very long period he did not like the painting, or at least thought it was too private to be shared, never showing it until a 1988 exhibition entitled *La couleur seule*, devoted to the monochrome, in the French city of Lyon. How different was the fate of *Train Landscape* (fig. 6), which he proudly included in his first New York show (at the Betty Parsons Gallery in 1956), as well as in his 1973 retrospective at the Museum of Modern Art! The contrast is all the more striking in that this latter work can be seen as Kelly's rectifying his course after the swerve, as if he were telling himself: "What was I thinking with this *Tableau Vert*?" Note that *Train Landscape* is based on a sketch that he made of a field of crops of various colors (lettuce, spinach, and mustard) seen from a train between Paris and Zürich, a coincidence (see note 1 above) that helps us imagine that it could be, at least at an unconscious level, another response to Monet.[6] *Train Landscape*, made of three monochrome panels, is in the quintessential impersonal, detached mode perfected by Kelly during his early years in Paris and governing his entire production to this day – as the recent *White Curve in Relief over White (Belle-Île)* of 2013 (cat. 29) reveals.

Fig. 6 Ellsworth Kelly, *Train Landscape*, 1953. Oil on canvas, three joined panels, 111.8 × 111.8 cm

One could even deem it an anti-Monet manifesto: no brushstroke, no color modulation, no mark of subjectivity whatsoever!

Train Landscape brings us to the second question this exhibition asks: What happens when an artist tries to put himself in the shoes of another, one whose entire aesthetic goes against the grain of his own? Let's start with the fact that this work is labeled a landscape only by virtue of its source material (a piling up of colors perceived on hills flanking the railroad tracks around Nancy). As a matter of fact, Kelly never painted a landscape properly speaking. (A student work called *Landscape with Doris* does not really qualify: next to the profile of his friend Doris is the view, from a balcony, of a tiny and sorry urban park adorned with a single tree.)[7] More importantly, he drew very few of them, comparatively speaking, after his return from the army in 1946. Most of his drawings and collages, thousands of them, are abstract. Parallel to those, which are in one way or another linked to his pictorial production, he did indeed make figurative drawings, several hundred of them, but the overwhelming majority are *portraits* of people or, as he says, of plants: the figure is isolated on the page, and there is no indication of its surroundings.[8] On the whole, there must be fewer than a hundred landscape drawings, produced in brief outbursts separated by long interruptions. (There are almost none between the handful made at Belle-Île in 1949 and those made when he returned to the island in 1965; then again, very few between 1965, the year during which he drew more than half of his landscapes, and 1975.) Most often, they partake more of the portrait mode than of anything else: they depict rock formations, inlets, watermarks on the beach, all seen at close range and once again without any information about their surroundings, which makes it impossible to gauge the scale of what is depicted. Often there is no horizon, no skyline, or – but then it is just as disorienting – the only thing that is depicted *is* the sky-line, as in a remarkable series of sketches he made in 1965 at Capri (fig. 7). That is to say: the landscape drawings presented in this exhibition are doubly exceptional, first being landscapes at all (since those are so rare in Kelly's graphic production) and then being landscapes that more or less conform to the tradition of the genre as exemplified by the pre-*Nymphéas* Monet. The coastal views in particular are exquisitely balanced, the spatial position of rocks is clearly rendered in perspective, the horizon firmly established: the beholder's point of view is secure. Only one of the sheets representing the rocks at Port-Coton is fully drawn in the "portrait" mode favored by Kelly (cat. 22). True, it contains some indication of depth, some overlapping and foreshortening, but nothing tells you that these forms are not those of stones scattered on the ground. Or, to give another example: compare the drawings done at the Plage Herlin that are included here (cats. 15 and 16) to others drawn at the same site and at the same time (also in 1965), depicting water-marks in the "portrait" mode just mentioned (fig. 8).

Fig. 7 Ellsworth Kelly, *Capri*, 1965. Ink on paper, 27.3 × 34.3 cm

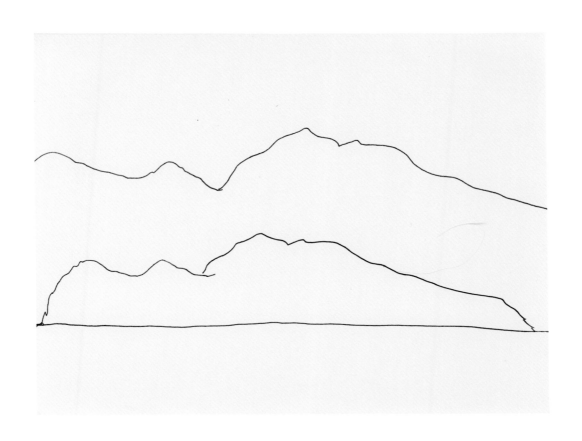

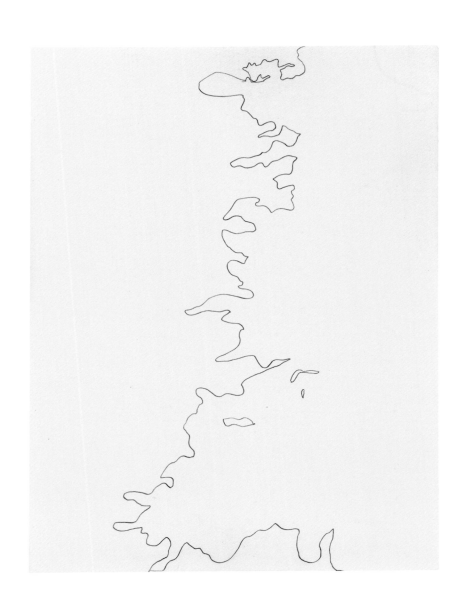

Did Kelly know that Monet had painted the rocks at Port-Goulphar when he went to Belle-Île in the summer of 1949, living for several months in a small fisherman's cottage just two miles from this site? This is far from certain. As a student of the Boston Museum School he had seen many works by Monet at the Museum of Fine Arts, Boston, but none are of the Breton scenery. The situation was very different when Kelly came back to Belle-Île in 1965 and even more so in 2005: then, just as he must have been thinking of Cézanne when drawing Mont Sainte-Victoire in 2000 (see cats. 17–21), he obviously had Monet in mind when sketching Port-Goulphar (cats. 27 and 28). The contrast is striking between those two dialogues with modernist masters. In the case of Aix painter, there is no dialogue per se; one could even speak of Kelly's resistance: it is as if his emphasis on contour could not blend with Cézanne's dictum that "there is no line."[9] Kelly's Mont Sainte-Victoire is so un-Cézannesque that one actually wonders if it is indeed the same mountain. Not so with regard to Monet: in the 1965 Belle-Île drawings included in this exhibition (except for the one mentioned above), Kelly seems to have had no difficulty joining Monet's serial game, juggling masses, and savoring the infinite variations of vistas to choose from, each different at every step one takes.

The 1949 drawings of the beach at Port-Donnant (cats. 10–13) are somewhat stiffer than all the later ones, or at least less assured, less nonchalant, but they were already, consciously or not, paying tribute to Monet's serial manner. However, what seems to have interested Kelly most as he climbed above the cove was the way in which the curve of a large rock at left almost touches – *à la* Michelangelo's *Creation of Adam* – the pointed edge of a cliff in the far distance, in a spatial short circuit that is actually much closer to Cézanne's way of thinking than to Monet's. (Such near contact of shapes would become a staple of Kelly's art.) As he was revisiting his sketchbooks in search of drawings to include in the current exhibition, *White Curve in Relief* happened to be hanging on the wall of his studio. After he stumbled upon the Port-Donnant sheets, it occurred to him that something vaguely similar was in play in this all-white work: the upper tip of the curve does not meet the horizontal edge of the panel, but almost. To the spatial conflation was added a temporal one: suddenly he saw himself marveling at the geographic drama of the Brittany coast. It is thus that *White Curve in Relief* was re-baptized *White Curve in Relief over White (Belle-Île)*.

Unlike everything else in this exhibition, *White Curve in Relief over White (Belle-Île)* does *not* represent an exception in Kelly's oeuvre, and its post-factum association with Monet in his mind was the result of fortuitous circumstances. Would this mean that, but for *Tableau Vert*, a work with no progeny in his oeuvre, Kelly had no use for Monet's pictorial production in his own? No direct use, certainly; but when are

Fig. 8 Ellsworth Kelly, *Water Mark, Plage Herlin (1)*, 1965. Pencil on paper, 54.6 × 41.9 cm

things ever direct? The *Nymphéas* he saw in Zürich and then in Giverny struck him as near-abstract paintings coming out of the experience of landscape, something that, for the most part, he had kept at bay in his artistic practice. *Tableau Vert* was Kelly's knee-jerk reaction to the visual shock he received in front of these enormous canvases. But *Train Landscape* was his more lasting response, for it dealt less with Monet's style than with the principle of creating an abstract work of art out of natural stimuli. Indeed, perhaps the fact that Monet's style was so different from his made it possible for Kelly to emulate him at a fundamental level while dodging any anxiety of influence.

1 See Ellsworth Kelly's *Artist's Statement* in this volume, 9. The statement was first published in *Monet and Modernism*, ed. Karin Sagner-Düchting, exh. cat. (Munich: Prestel, 2001), 214. As Kelly mentions in the same statement, he had actually already seen some large water-lily paintings by Monet: at the Zürich Kunsthaus in May 1952 – and that was the initial shock that eventually led to the Giverny visit. Indeed, two large *Nymphéas* canvases, given by Emil Georg Bührle to the Zürich Kunsthaus in 1952 were included in the Monet retrospective held that very year in the museum from 10 May to 17 July. Those, however, are more "populated" (and less "all-over") than some of the works he saw at Giverny a few months later.

2 He also noted their formidable size (in itself an object of admiration but also of envy, given his material impossibility at the time to carry out his desire to work at a mural scale).

3 Stella mocked this tradition in a famous interview that Bruce Glaser made of him and his minimalist comrade Donald Judd ("you do something in one corner and you balance it with something in the other corner"). See Bruce Glaser, "Questions to Stella and Judd," in *Minimal Art: A Critical Anthology*, ed. Gregory Battcock (New York: E. P. Dutton, 1968), 149.

4 See Michael Leja, "The Monet Revival and New York School Abstraction," in *Monet in the Twentieth Century*, Paul Hayes Tucker et al., exh. cat. (Boston: Museum of Fine Arts; London: Royal Academy of Arts, 1998), 98–108.

5 Kelly, in *Monet and Modernism*, 214.

6 Kelly identified the crops in a conversation with Trevor J. Fairbrother. See Fairbrother, *Ellsworth Kelly: Seven Paintings (1952–55/1987)*, exh. cat. (Boston: Museum of Fine Arts, 1987).

7 In his vast pictorial production, Kelly explicitly identified only seven works as landscapes. After *Landscape with Doris* came three paintings from 1950, consisting of black lines on a white ground, based on "automatic" doodles (*Romantic Landscape* [EK 16], *Medieval Landscape* [EK 17], and *City Landscape* [EK 24]: hardly plein-air vistas!). *Train Landscape* was painted in 1953, but then one has to wait until 1958 for *West Coast Landscape Study* (EK 137), enlarged two years later in *West Coast Landscape* (EK 259) – both consisting of four irregular horizontal bands of, from top to bottom, blue, green, black, and red.

8 "My drawings are really *portraits* of plants, starting with the stem, the branches, the leaves, and maybe sometimes the flowers." Marla Prather, "Interview with Ellsworth Kelly," in *Ellsworth Kelly: Plant Drawings: 1948–2010*, exh. cat., ed. Marla Prather and Michael Semff (Munich: Schirmer/Mosel, 2011), 213.

9 Paul Cézanne, quoted by Émile Bernard in 1904. This translation from Michael Doran, ed., *Conversations with Cézanne* (Berkeley and London: University of California Press, 2001), 38.

Kelly
Paintings and Drawings

10
Plage de Port-Donnant
1949
Pencil on paper, 33 × 45.7 cm

Works are collection of the artist
unless otherwise noted

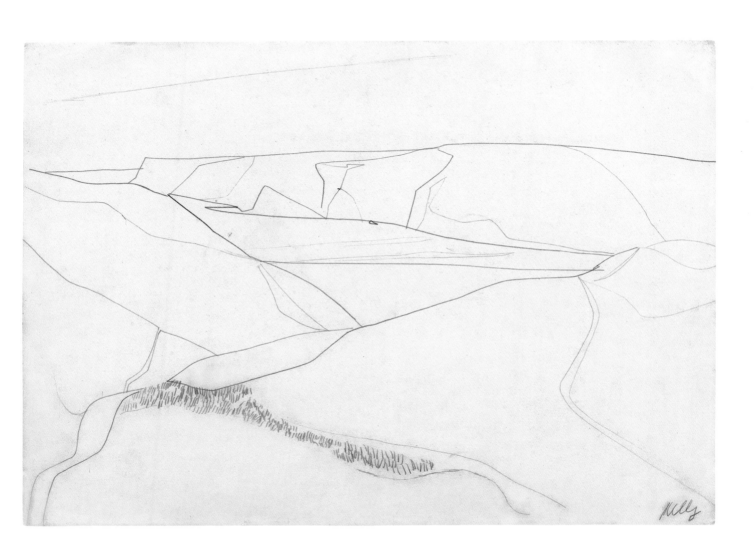

11
Plage de Port-Donnant
1949
Pencil on paper, 33 × 45.7 cm

Following pages

12
Plage de Port-Donnant
1949
Pencil on paper, 21 × 26.7 cm

13
Plage de Port-Donnant
1949
Pencil on paper, 21 × 26.7 cm

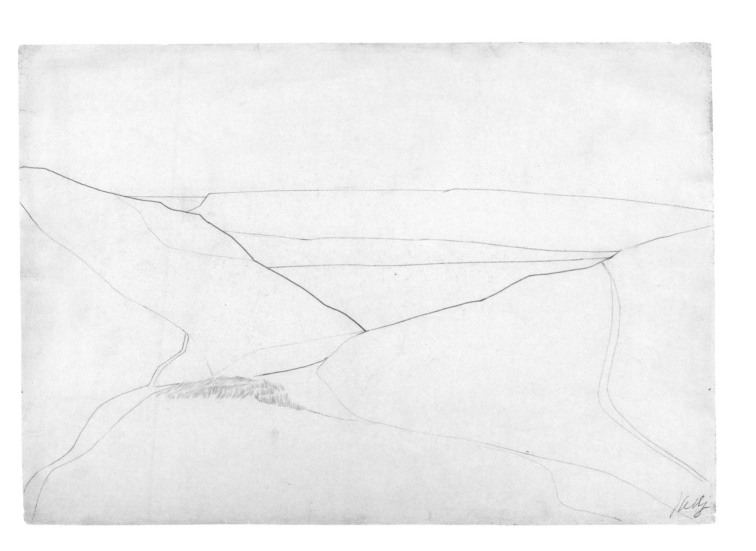

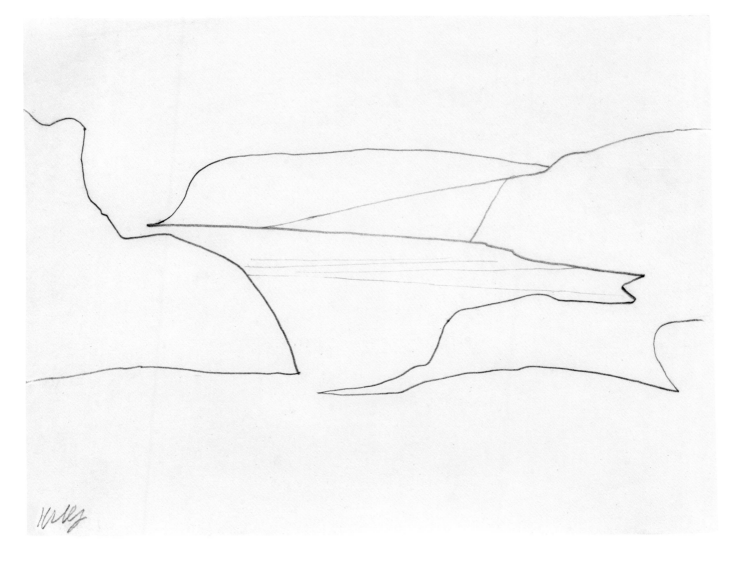

14
Tableau Vert
1952
Oil on wood, 74.3 × 99.7 cm
The Art Institute of Chicago
Gift of the artist

PORT-COTON, BELLE-ILE   JUNE 05

29
*White Curve in Relief over White
(Belle-Île)*
2013
Oil on canvas, two joined panels,
120 × 213.4 cm

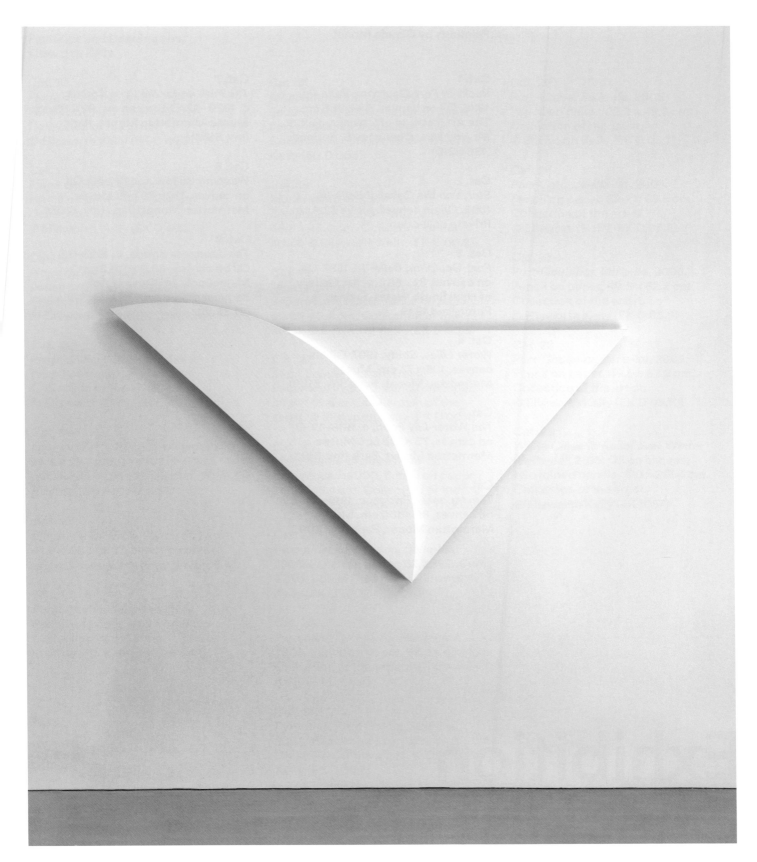

Photography Credits